Rattus Rattus

PETER ROSE grew up in country Victoria. After studying at Monash University and working as a bookseller, he moved to Oxford University Press and was a publisher there throughout the 1990s. He is currently the Editor of *Australian Book Review*. His first collection of poetry, *The House of Vitriol*, appeared in 1990, and was followed by *The Catullan Rag* (1993) and *Donatello in Wangaratta* (1998). His poetry and criticism have appeared in various anthologies. In 2001 he published a memoir, *Rose Boys*, which won several prizes, including the National Biography Award. His first novel, *A Case of Knives*, will appear in 2005.

Rattus Rattus

NEW AND SELECTED POEMS

PETER ROSE

SALT

CAMBRIDGE

PUBLISHED BY SALT PUBLISHING
PO Box 937, Great Wilbraham, Cambridge PDO CB1 5JX United Kingdom

First published 2005

Printed and bound in the United Kingdom by Lightning Source

Typeset in Swift 9.5 / 13

ISBN 1 84471 069 6 paperback

Australian Government

*This project has been assisted by the Australian Government
through the Australia Council, its arts funding and advisory body.*

1 3 5 7 9 8 6 4 2

To Christopher Menz

Contents

Acknowledgments

Acknowledgments are due to the editors of the following publications, in which the poems collected in *Rattus Rattus* first appeared:

The Age, *Antipodes* (USA), *Atlanta Review* (USA), *Australian's Review of Books*, *Canberra Times*, *Heat*, *Island*, *Meanjin*, *Metre* (Ireland), *Overland*, *Southerly*, *Stand* (UK), *Verse* (USA) and *The Weekend Australian*.

Several of the poems from 'The Catullan Rag' first appeared in *The Best Australian Poems* 2003. 'Morning Bias' was reprinted in *The Best Australian Poetry* 2003 and 'U-Bahn' in *The Best Australian Poetry* 2004. 'Rattus Rattus', 'The Calling of St Matthew' and 'Hospital of the Innocents' first appeared in *Time's Collision with the Tongue*; and 'Mildura, 2003' and 'Anthem for Jurors' in *Vintage: Celebrating Ten Years of the Mildura Writers' Festival*. An earlier version of 'Quotidian' appeared in a *Salt Anthology*.

I am grateful to Arts South Australia for a grant which helped me to write *Rattus Rattus* and several poems in 'The Catullan Rag'. My thanks also go to Chris Emery and John Kinsella at Salt Publishing.

New Poems

Late Edition

Most things are never meant.
PHILIP LARKIN, 'Going, Going'

Midnight. A collision threatens
to happen. Sally of breaks.
It procrastinates like an aria,
teasing night editors with their cigarettes.
May never culminate. Interest wanes.
Ignoring the unskilled night
I resume the book of memoirs.
Name-dropping is his genius.
We know each footnote in our
anonymous eyries.
                    Again, midnight.
Pedestrians, ubiquitous in scarves,
hasten to the equivocal accident,
never sure what it will disclose.
The cathedral stands idle,
bells strung up like colanders.
Silence. Never such silence.
In another part of the house
you sleep on, oblivious —
dreams that may or may not happen.

Morning Bias

for John Slade

Crab-like, immaculate,
millionth rollie in his mouth,
the septuagenarian dreams
on his buggy, pressing
ancient greenery before
advent of bowlers in white.
Velvet of ages in a reverie,
soft implicit morning.
Shadows on the green
inch like natural biases.
Flags go up: imperial.
Weekdays bring Apollos
in pinstripes and brogues,
but Saturday souls
are serious as hats.
A car door slams shut,
heralding the first quip.
Old men in white appear:
creased, defiant, stooped.
All week they have spun balls
in the mind, anticipating
the edging out of friends.
Old jokes are passed
like pikelets on a plate.
A new hip is welcomed
to the brotherhood of joints.
Glinting in the sun, a coin
pirouettes and disappoints.

Rope

Oddly moving,
this coiling of hands on a tram,
public ropery
in the swept world.

Sunset happens
in the temples and atriums;
old men peel
anarchic posters from a wall.

Solutions are scrawled
on this our nothingness.
Voices soften—
and the veiled threat.

Escalator

In the dream there is neither
wishing nor deserving.
We move through loveless lobbies,
soviet emporia of the mind,
greet our anguished fathers,
recognizably unrecognizable,
load our brothers on the forlorn slope,
only to bundle them up again
at the foot of the dream,
oblivious to our stratagems,
our needfulness—
naked, contestable, alone.

Ladybird

For my brother

One year ago almost to the hour
we got the news about our father
and it was downhill all the way,
six weeks of crisp mordacity.
No quarter-century lessening for him:
just a curt sentence and eclipse.

Yes, one year ago, almost to the hour.
Except you weren't there,
dead yourself these five years—
on your daughter's birthday.
You never understood my lexical craze
but I could spend eternity hunting for a
long beautiful word for addicts of anniversaries.
There must be a name for it, a need.

Five years. No time, but all time:
lustrum of encyclopedic loss.
You were twenty-two when it happened;
forty-seven at your death, younger than I am.
Why is it that only now do I feel
the full burden of its grotesquerie,
the callous moral heft of it—
not those bulky limbs we lifted
and straightened a thousand times,
but the early loss of you, the spasmic curse?

And still I go on reading:
for distraction or enlightenment.
Today I'm deep in Gosse's *Father and Son*,
so numb at the horrors of the Brethren
I put myself to sleep quite deliberately—
for thirteen minutes, my watch tells me
when I stir. Well, my father's watch.
Our mother slipped it off his wrist as he lay dying

and handed it to me, consolation in time.
'Not that it's worth much,' she said,
reminiscing about the notorious clip
that always failed him at critical moments.
Collingwood veterans still laugh about it,
how it was always coming undone
during halftime speeches. They'd wait
for Dad to punch his fist for emphasis.
Now it brings me undone too,
during meetings or writing this poem.
Often it dangles down or pinches me,
like a warning, a reminder.

Suddenly I'm dreaming on my bed.
It is a cursory dream, a digest from the dark,
sharp as the flick that wrenched your neck,
your birthright, your physicality.

Thirteen minutes. It feels longer—
curdling a long life into an hour.
That's how long our tennis matches took.
We'd set off on Sunday afternoons,
always fretting about the weather.
You weren't playing, of course.
Patient in your wheelchair, you'd umpire
by the net, laughing at our squabbles,
our limp trademark backhands.

Today, though, in my dream,
it's you I'm competing against—
though the court resembles my bedroom
with its monographs and cityscape.
The game is tense and visceral.
Neither of us bothers to remark
that you're nimble again, competitive.

Tense as compasses we hunt down balls
and eye each line like jealous colonizers.
When your deft backhand hits a corner
I'm about to call it out until I notice
a damp mark on the en tout cas—rather,
my pallid carpet, which shows every stain.
With queasy sportsmanship I call it in
and we play on. I lose the point.
Next game, I watch my nervous backhand
miss by an inch and am surprised when
you hunt it down. But your cross-court shot
misses by feet and seconds later you call 'Out'—
meaning mine. 'A bit late!' I pout,
trudging back and sinking into clay
which oozes now and swallows me,
this high bedroom become a mire.
So the tubercular diva splutters on her deathbed,
impatient for a word. *E tardi.*
I await your response but wake too soon.
The contest is over, always unfinished.
I cannot will it back, resume the game.
Too late, indeed. We leave it much too late.

Yet when I take up my Gosse —
one anniversary over, another to come —
what do I find but a ladybird
creeping over the yellowing Penguin
and settling on my father's watch.
I haven't seen one since Wangaratta.
Straight as an arrow it takes me back
to the bridge we played beneath as boys,
dumping our bikes by the road.
Teasing each other, we'd compete
to find the most ladybirds,
rapt, jostling each other, ecstatic.

Quotidian

Summer and open doors.
Sore throats dry as cepous tanks.
Serpents multiply, worrying about—
not language this time but how
to holiday in a figurative skin.
Before collapse the condition
must be beautiful. Extraneous noises
whether burglar or rodent rattling a pane
bring exchange students seeking
not verification this time
but something to open the wine.
We stammer and splutter
and soar through the roof.
Traffic shuffles its pack.
Manuscripts mate in the rushes—
Adored Allergies, Everyman's Book of Incest.
Lifting carpets they bring us
booty from a bombed Society.
Acrid are those air-conditioned rumours:
her voice quite shot above the stave.
A clinician's sleek phrasing.
Jars of lemon butter
which a grandmother saved.
Or so they said, and open doors.
I remember her vaguely
but not her condiments,
only someone removing her dentures
as in a morality play. We visit
the dead with appalled compliments,
testing upholstery. What frightened me
across that still acre,
everyone's portcullis down?
Panic marches on parliament
giving interviews. On television
the febrile conductor

dies for hourly bulletins,
serial ravages mining his brow,
but they go out with rutting pandas
and the theme from *Hair*.
Summer and open doors.

Homage

How eloquent you found it,
a stray gesture recalled one evening
as we sat in that obscure inn we liked.
You'd met her at a party not long before.
She was older, Spanish, a sculptor.
Though it wasn't a literary affair
you began extolling the poetry of Cavafy,
which we'd just been reading.
I could imagine the charming way
you'd introduced it, the softness
in your voice, the effect.
At first she said nothing, moved,
then she placed one hand on her breast,
impressing you with her dignity,
her understatement. Needless to say,
I made a lengthy note in my journal,
putting down everything.
Some time later, the poet's name
again being mentioned,
I repeated her gesture, thinking
you would have forgotten its provenance—
who had forgotten much else.
Immediately the gesture felt false, wooden,
not even Spanish. Either you were
too tactful to remark on my faux pas
or failed to notice, but I knew,
lowering a foreign abject unavailing hand.

Last Words

Voices twining in the valley of evening.

Benisons of summer
late and beguiling.

Getting just so far
or where you were
by the appointed hour.

Shadow, murmur, interstice.

Consolations of the pantry
radiant with marmalade,
all she ever made.

Fond cheque-book rippling in the sun.

Watching the smile
melt on her fascinated face
as noticed but unnoticing he passed.

Cape of temerity.
Silk of *Schadenfreude*.

Behind each bookcase, musty betrayals in manuscript.

The Governors of the Feast

Things of beauty even.
What do you say to that now, brash boy?
Show me your big collective teeth.
Cigarize those banknotes on your thighs.
Give me your lust, your empery.
It will hold up sure as morning and imperfect.
Communal laundries tinkle in the frost,
the way a high-rise manoeuvres
through cloudscape, eclipses it.
A shudder passes through the capital:
love moved them and made them print.
Brokers of the perfect oracle
tender for a colonnade. They have forgotten
everything about themselves and smile.
A Greek god deliberately snubs
my better half, emulsive cut.
There is chattering, more vitriol.
They will bury that story forever,
seal it in tar and gloss the prince.
The governors of the feast welcome us
in a thousand hefty languages.
Everything they wear matches ruthlessly:
costume jewellery, amoral studs.
Now only the children and their usurers,
warped victories of calligraphy.

Rattus Rattus

Even at midnight
the pontiff's window is open,
framing the next blessing or admonition.

Combing the colonnade
late tourists shop for symbols.

In the square
a thousand chairs
pray to a vacant altar.

Chesty bells convulse a dozen times.
'Electric', you mutter.

Amputees put away
their disabilities and dream.

Handsome carabinieri
erect barriers to Bernini's scheme.

Beside each column
a metal detector
radiates our nothingness.

Following the Tiber home,
footsore and fascinated,
we watch a stupendous rat,
bigger than a monstrance,
mapping the slimy historic bank.

The Calling of St Matthew
for Christopher

Pensive for the dramas of paid light,
tourists loiter in a pew fingering strange currency,
not unlike the striped youth in Caravaggio's view
who alone misses the drama, hidden by a fetching fringe.
Tithes on a table captivate and multiply.
When someone sacrifices a coin to San Luigi's rattle
we crane to appreciate, and will it to last and last.
Darkness is what we fear in our aesthetic march:
the psychiatrist with his father's satchel,
brow furrowed after a hot day's frankness;
an aged *inglese* slumped on her collapsible,
which she hauls across Europe like a pilgrim,
limping from Annunciation to Deposition,
hardly approving of a squalid Virgin in the Louvre;
or that handsome woman with the dancer's gait
who goes straight to the Contarelli Chapel
but only to read the misspelt notes
(Trust become a Truss: we are in Rome),
as if to peer would be to discompose
what this sideburned Christ enjoins.
Meanwhile the fashionable congregation
swells and leaves, swells and leaves,
clutching its Walkmans, its talismans.
No one listens to the loquacious guide.
He is outside this charismatic square,
reduces all Rome's vaults to a single hermitage,
coffered, domed, a terrible *trompe l'oeil*.
As the last lira slips away a woman sighs profoundly
as if half-pitying our tax collector in his new shocked light,
remembering some tall beseecher from her past.
Just then, entranced, I remember my own vocation
and slip past Caravaggio's pierced worshippers,
past the amputee baring his pink stump

(too garish for Western charity),
and meet you as arranged in Sant'Agostino,
where undisturbed we illuminate another frank calling.

Hospital of the Innocents

Approach it as you would any alien idea or equestrian statue,
that bronze scourge astride a placid epiphany,
ruthless and medalled in a gypsied piazza,
near a foundling hospital where the downcast chip away at their lives,
leave them sleeping on flagstones like original scandals.
The moon is available and besmirched as any duomo.
Why not climb the cupola if your head can cope?
The Last Judgment has been restored for us,
the company, the coterie, never so inviting. Let's study
the hips of passing saints for signs of loveliness, a monogram.
We have surely met that concierge before, Judas in beige.
Nothing ages in an inflationary future.
But too many vistas, too much East Coast journalism altogether.
They will edit my archness and offer crostini
(which you, lunging across a table, trailing something
diaphanous in oil, will insist upon tasting).
Best not travel when a legend expires:
the footpaths are full of it—it suffocates.
What's in a life anyway? asks the famous biographer,
too savvy for stringy sympathy.
We come to forget our polar association,
though it perforce jolts in the memoried Campo.
Try describing Uluru after several grappas.
Why, it was the evening you gave up smoking—
fondly I recall your fevered protestations.
The last duomo is the most pensive, the most devout.
Couples study each other for signs of imminent apostasy,
stepping over a Massacre of the Innocents.
Facing rows of popes' heads, corrupt as stone,
swivel like gargoyles in a place of skulls.
You pay more to go into the library, coinage spilling in the chapel.
As the final crocodile winds from the chipped allegory
a Franciscan, worthy of a winking three-dimensional postcard,

enrobes for the nightly miracle, ignoring us.
I drift around unveiling new terrible stigmata
while flawless orphans coltishly sightsee.

The Prize

How intently we esteem the prize
depends on ropes of shadow beside the Elbe
and wiles of clamorous currents
that beguile late oarsmen in their throes.
Mozart, nearing death, told Constanze
that what he savoured in the stalls
was the approving silence, not applause.
So we all linger on a chord and will it
not to end—until the maniac bravo.
In my rusticated dream all that wafts
towards us is a relic of tourism,
an assiduous cuckoo loyal to its vineyard.
They were serving this Müller-Thurgau
long before Meissen or art nouveau.
Imagine crossing the slicked historical river
and conquering other interiors of the self,
ones long boarded up and forgotten,
oblivious to blandishments of the sun,
the silvered city's vitiating notes.

U-Bahn

They are not cannibalizing yet,
those lowered voices.
A sidelong glance out of Dürer
perfects the new vocation, a bitter tense.
Faces pressed too closely
as in a holy family skirmish
avert their gaze,
sepiaed and equivocal.
The Italian boy who is all lash
whispers in a foreign sleep.

Afternoon at the Huntington

Deep into memory I go,
deep as an insidious shadow
inching across an expensive room
briefly occupied by heirless dilettantes.

Art on a wall
is wavous and obscure.
Inscrutable, it seems,
is all we ever feel.

Across the room you bring me
in mellow undertones
the essential quotation—
both intimate and never crisply learned.

Keith Jarrett: The Second Concert

Backstage,
slumped in amaze,
towel round your neck
like a heavyweight champ,
you are circled by jazz fiends,
pirate recordists and local arrivistes,
a blind prodigy led by the hand.
One cat farewells you saying,
'I'll see you in Japan.'
Another wants to know
what applause feels like,
as if it's a disease
reserved for the nimble.
Above the din I hear you ask,
'Man, when was the last time
you went deep sea diving?
The ocean is not the waves.
First there is silence,
then boredom, only then music.'

Caveat

I master you like a slow equestrian portrait,
the masterpiece with permanent guard,
brutally restored and never to be toured,
never quite owned by nation or industrialist,
priceless so they say in the catalogue raisonné.
Your provenance snakes through dubious dynasties:
bankers purloined you, then a White Russian.
Your student, I commit you to memory,
sly perspectives and iconography,
what every drake and strawberry plumply signify.
It is christian but also fleshy, omnivorous,
excites the only epigram in my repertoire,
the sole sure phrase in years of war.
Though I shun the ring of dilettantes
I long to hear them praise your brushwork,
cloudy distances of grey and pearl,
the way you draw me into your orbit, your *sfumato*.

Sentence

Tell me the worst now
while the sun is shining
and the children rowdily homing
with their pesky instruments.
Tell me what you have in mind
while day is still defined enough
to dabble in. I shall wait by that tree
until it blazes up in its futility.
I shall memorize a sonnet backwards
as a thespian reins his burdened mind.
Tell me what you have assigned
with your senators. Stop at nothing:
the grammar of their prejudice,
how they flippantly phrased it,
the clinical light euphemistic, shuddering.

Bespoke Night

And then, astonished,
remembering it was bird
tutored in the uppermost,
the shadow rose up,
tottered in its brace of wing,
all our passaging denied.
Grass scorching before our eyes,
everything lay flattened,
pure pelt—disclosures
of fig, an historic thong.

Graffiti

Catching our breath, patterned by unseasonableness,
we feel it simultaneously, the way indifference
envelops a restaurant like a peace conference,
fresh shows of bigotry in a literary grove.
They are with us, they shadow us, stepping
out of ourselves. My old stark repertoire
does things to your complexion.
Would you go back in time, in thought, in place?
How do you feel about a dig on an afternoon
resolute as this: sunshine, tangerines,
auguries of captivated night?
Not quite as unpredictable, don't you think?
We have all witnessed that thrashing,
evasions of dark. We have been up
those stairs so many times numeracy
invades our joints. Home, so private
we are nameless, we find them raising glasses
in a timeless toast. We draw the blinds,
prospect for inner worlds, we agitate for tremors.

Exorbitant Confession

Then someone's demanding to know
how this behemoth gets into our dreams,
as if so-and-so's shiny nose, in the Fulfilment Department,
infiltrates our nights—just watch!
Axed by fax, colleagues are counselled in our rites.
Your response is so much braggadocio,
slithering through cyberspace to adjust a blind.
Even motes are terrified at times,
while all we do is menace the air
with our mornings and our distempers,
worse for the temp spraying coffee on a carpet.
The best we can offer is a perch
in our crummiest photograph, the last decapitable inch.
It's not true what the moralists said—it never was.
Easy to resolve marriages into the photogenic
and the frankly plain, the agonized.
If he still manages to be sunny
the bent one's bound to be refined.
In the dream the whole tribe is spreading over spurs, plains,
down devastated gullies, sites of penultimate massacres,
affording no glimpse of the chiliastic screen.
Life, like *Ben Hur*, recurs on alternate nights,
each saturated frame arresting us like awed ushers.

Bridal

In the rear vision mirror
the bride and groom seem mute,
pinned there at traffic lights.
Her silk is quiet as a vow,
his posture a little stooped.
Married too early at midday?
Midday passes, and the restaurants.
Stepping from any limousine
he might resume his life,
the tortive weather.
In the front, her parents
are garrulous and miss the lights.
No one prompts them,
the graphic couple destined and still.

To Adelaide

Dawn flights weave eccentric routes,
veering as the land balds,
holdings scarred and beautiful.
Sunlight dawdles on a dam,
ignites the midget fauna.
Apologizing for our tardiness
the pilot says we are bearers
of spare parts for a stricken jet.
'What sort of an excuse is that?'
bawls my Texan neighbour.
Below, the land is quilted
like a chequered past,
cosmetic, infinitely private.
The in-flight service is delayed
and I am glad, but not the Americans.
Just as the captain predicts
a smooth flight we hit the turbulence.

Sheep at Dookie

A hundred yards away they sense me,
stir from green gluttony,
tremulous and panic-struck,
unused to idlers on country roads
in their veils of dust.
When I pass they are huddled
in a corner of the field,
a sorry, leaderless revolt.
Forever at right angles,
they gawk at what I signify
or fail to signify.
A magpie swoops the ancient air,
ignores me. Like the sender
of some slow telegraph
a mudlark pogoes down a fence,
always a few yards ahead,
fastidious, unshy.
Opposite all our zoology
a field of canola shudders
for bronze omens of the sun.

Murray Drift

How they drift, those tanned boys
with their feet in the water,
leggy gargoyles of the ludic houseboat.
As it purrs they bluely stare,
the green Murray a purling future,
cool, snaking, ancestral,
always bringing something round the bend,
if only tourists rocking
a pink motor boat called *Lipstick*.
Beyond snags and rip, a scalloped beach.
Someone swam there once,
or was it another cove?
Certainty roves in a floating future.
Intricate eucalypt shadows
inch across sand towards river,
slip into fathomless water, dissolve.

Balnarring Beach

Summer, late afternoon breezes,
a green sail nervously aloft.
Siblings in pink togs
hurdling waves, quashing them.
A moment's rivalry frantic
as tears, soon mollified.
Battles with wind-breaks,
a congratulatory calm
soon disappointing.
Unaccustomed nods to strangers,
a little astonished.
Too much seaweed, I guess,
but souvenired for mulch.
Ebullient games of cricket
in the sea, ranging
the whitest of cordons,
sly snicks into surf.
Beyond the point,
cool vistas in a hushed cove,
the lovers' eyeful colloquy.
Intermittent squalls,
elders sheltering in a cliff.
Pungent rocks luring
fascinated canines, philosophers.
The facing island, a mortal blue,
beckons, intensifies, vanishes.

Mildura, 2003

Through the Grand's frosted glass
two pigeons in silhouette,
their dislocating rites
tender theatre on a sill.

That coo will run through my weekend,
a cure for solity—
the insolence of being left,
noticing each weft in the tapestry.

I've come ahead.
Your plane is late, as if on time.
Sometimes the one himself
cannot avail.

Rain unwonted as crops
has locals gaping.
After the formalities
we all go down to the river in shifts.

Posthumous Jazz

Opposite,
garbled whoops,
a shot voice arrests itself.

Night speeds up, injects,
assesses the effect,
everything percussive, mere drum.

Hypnotically veined,
he rejects sleep,
tan hands for elusive gods.

The remnants of modesty
are fanned by a revised breeze,
musicked with auguries.

The Glittering Prize

Ever dissolving, day is bedimmed by officialdom,
reminds us to check our cloaks in the conscience room.
It's milky out there, sombre as Cazneaux's wood.
Soon night will anoint itself and we will all be there,
shiny, not a fraction late. You have your pass:
represent yourself as darkly as only you know how.
There are as many standards as logos in this twisting world.
Trust me: you will suck strawberries white as a juror
and hear bateless talk about the viscous process,
intrigue bobbling on the terrace—hissy fits from Leviticus.
The foyer is draped with Olive Cottons and Yoko's coffins,
macabre as children. By threads of reputation
gossamer hangs from an elevated egg,
'translucent' ringings in our head. Fondling his name-tag,
the guard with his vest of secrets ignores
the Ukrainian outcast wielding his member.
Grandmothers usher legatees into a darkened room,
encouraging the prodigies to annotate this mire.
Quaint to find cardigans in such a needled world.

Ivan Ilyich

Radical eye on the book of death.
Curtains—he insists—yes, curtains
of a certain tawdriness
motion to him of their own accord.
The useless cord dangles like a cure, a noose.
'Why have I lived?'
Words adjudicate in florid robes.
A piano is removed but memory plays
ghosts of cheerless sarabands.
A hireling looms and polishes the air.
Suns of subjectivity quiver in the glass.
Tulips appear in prissy rows,
timid voices in the hallway—
phrases of the unavailing sacrament.

Dirigible

Somewhere, I suppose, a waking
is celebrated, wine poured,
tokens exchanged.

Here, balloons hang
like absorbed satellites,
golden, unmanned.

Anthem for Jurors

Yes, they will say this for him, despite what you think.
They will have a phrase for every condition,
mint new words for his discomfiture.
Provocatively they remember, misremember,
never forgetting a certain anniversary, the drift of it.
With histrionic flair and diction they intone:
how he rose without trace, once nearly died,
whom he thoughtlessly married and discarded.
They interview the erstwhile wife, they film her.
Speculation gathers around him, fertile as imprudent thought:
a minor blemish say, whether cutaneous or subcutaneous,
something fraying round the edges of a life,
the way an aphorism fails to ignite a table,
leaving him exposed and subtly tongue-tied,
however facile, however languid in the linen suit
they deprecate in their matted commentaries.
Journals flower with bitter blossom,
though now and then they venture a compliment,
sure of his ultimate vanquishment.
Never knowing why, too highly strung for lieder,
eschewing galleries where they once moved freely,
breathed freely, meeting lovers in surreal loggias,
leading them through rooms to a certain gouache—
never quite sure why, they listen for disparate sounds,
telling oratorios of something shattering.
In their rising impatience, the moon never sufficing,
they rarely look up, dress less fastidiously,
lose the feeling in their limbs like widowed queens.
Subscriptions are allowed to lapse, old music never played.
But never so lucid, never so perspicuous.
Though they cannot adduce arcane philosophies
they remain opinionated and deeply sceptical.
In dreams never so vivid or feudal
they exchange cards with discredited autocrats,
anoint him with the bile of their regard.

Lacking the vocabulary, they never enquire about an absence.
When it arises in magazines they look away embarrassed,
eager for the tribulation they know must come—
justice of the vituperative. And when it does,
luminous, graphic, they will circle him, agape.
Until when, they drop him lines, include him in millennial revels—
in wilder moments, bored or disgusted, even insinuate themselves
in his bed, tantalizing him, inardent, becoming him.

The House of Vitriol (1990)

The Wound

I was there when it happened,
the night you cut yourself, marred
those peerless hands on a specious blade.
No doubt you won't remember.
Memory is a solipsist, inhabits
a white room with frayed blinds,
unable to conceive the witness
of our clumsiness. But I was there,
unknown, invisible, just a voice,
an invitation. I saw it coming,
could have averted it even.
It was summer, nightfall,
the sun's red lit upon a wall,
in your glass the rank lees settled.
Wearied by intrigue, commerce, guests,
your usual dexterity abandoned you;
with a gleam the long knife fell
across your hand, silvering a slash.
Not sadism nor waywardness rooted
me there, the romantic clinician.
The outcome was never in doubt.
Nothing serious. No cicatrice.
This was the driest wound.
The driest wound. What mortified
was your rage, your indignation,
hurling the blade across a room,
taunting fate with a gaping hand.
This was hubris, noblesse;
this was more than pride,
which no one suspected until the
eve of devastation. Pride, audacity,
those magnificent hands. No blood to run.

Alsatian Traveller

How lone she looked
on the back seat,
grizzled, vice-regal
like a dowager aunt
driven through suburbs,
troubled by what she saw,
a disappearing universe
gone mad with dispassion,
shorn youth with razored noses,
anti-heroines trailing
Edwardian fashions,
the sadness of ancients
craning for trams.

Mortification

I am walking down a classroom.
It is always the same, only longer,
the chalked message on the board
become daily more blurred.
On my right the good sit
unctuous hands crossed primly,
to my left the incorrigible
sailing their furtive orgasms
like the first kites of sex.
At the front a certain Mr Bull
instructs us in the gorier aspects
of devotion. History titillates
with Great Character Assassinations.
Follows recess: the lacteous spill.
Too blithe to matter, we are let out
to contemplate Lady Godiva *ad nauseam*
while great Samurai crazes give way
to mass flayings of the unconscionable.
We pair off beneath trees
and kill off aunts conversationally.

Prime Minister's Grandson

Hermetic, bloodless, solitary,
enemy of gossip and galumphing athleticism,
thin and morbid as a Byzantine,
seen only ever in profile,
habitué of dramatic quads,
born wearer of tragic scarves,
always several genres ahead of us
(Knut, Kafka, Kerouac, *Steppenwolf*),
said to have been born in France
and to hold multiple passports,
delicate as Sèvres porcelain,
accorded the status of a junior master,
beyond chastisement and economics,
known never to watch television
and to esteem only Wagner,
devotee of rancid cheese:
you we christened our Black Prince.
Not for you the hysteria of the hockey field,
Prussian capers of Cadets,
Tuesdays found you practising topiary,
entertaining coteries of widows
solicitous of your health.
Otherwise you never spoke,
spurning all Tory acolytes,
though rumour had you destined for
the stage. If my Sikes forgot his lines
your pubescent Oliver was magniloquent.
One lunchtime I heard you reading
Hamlet to the blackboard's Gertrude.
Coined for commerce or clapped-out poetry
we knew you would make a better
actor than your grandfather,
who loomed in a Rolls to dispense
calf-bound Eliot and sense.
True vocation was a rarity that year:

two chefs, a priest, an engineer—
was it respect or fear that chilled us?
Years later, reading the memoirs
of Vyvyan Holland, I picture
you again, a kind of outcast:
friendless, rootless, circumspect,
baritonal orphan of the gods.

Pathology

Because I am not prolific

Because I was never invited
into the Sacristy of Art,
but hung round foyers
bitching about syntax

Because the boy at the door recognized me,
but in the wrong context

Because my footsteps in the corridor
are stealthy, obsequious

Because I never married a bronchial woman with bad taste

Because I was led up a Golden Staircase
by a cicerone trailing fire

Because my address
is unfashionable nothingness,
a cobalt square in which nothing happens,
not even nature

Because I was never baptized

Because I was guilty of making disrespectful noises
in the Pantheon of Imagining
with its pay phones and baldaquins

Because I long ago eschewed wristwatches

Because the priest in the confessional
spoke always the wrong language

Because I give decent, boring dinner parties

Because as a youth
I was too easily flattered
by *roués* in Chevrolets

Because my excuses are my memories,
and vice versa

Because, held captive in the Monumental City,
I lost all reason,
dipped my camera in the holy water

Because there was never enough seating in the plaza

Because my follies were legion,
my faux pas threefold
at the Great Cocktail Party

Because I am always several things,
never one

Because the dove bludgeoned
excites neither pity not revulsion

Because,
in a trance of metamorphic love,
I preferred the company of beggars

Because this poems alters nothing—

For these and excellent other reasons
I know we are condemned
to sit throughout the night,
waiting for dawn
to wash the leaves white

And I know of brutish faces
gavotting in the mind,
exploited and refined,
to be sold everywhere,
on street corners,
in miniature

Terminus

The whorl inside my head buzzes,
this cog which no one can replicate.
Somewhere you lie dying,
given till midnight.
You fell down on a tram,
blacked out between terminals,
fit, bright, twenty-one.
Puccini gave Manon an aria
but it hardly seems to matter much.
No doubt they shrank
from your devastating touch,
ricking their necks
in an effort not to look,
just as I, unable to fathom
this ruin, this mystery,
this topical egg,
pause for a moment
before going on with
my reread novel, my TLS.

Memorabilia

So, finally, what have I kept of yours,
what buried to remember you by?
For a start, philosophic ditties
of doubtful provenance,
boxfuls of old elusive letters,
a morose photograph of you as Hamlet.
(You stayed up all night to develop it.)
Wrapped in our sheet,
absolutely cheerless and profound,
those lips might be cankered I have kissed,
the proud mouth a slash of desolation.
Cryptic Anno Dominis follow,
taunting the bearer of the key-shaped card:
Hitler's rise or a Happy Majority?
More prized, a pea-soupy edition of *La Nausée*,
next to Volume Two of de Beauvoir's memoirs,
Sartre's longiloquent love.
I remember, you stole them for me
at an English bookshop near the Spanish Steps.
Coward that I am, I watched you stuff them
down walking boot and trouser leg,
petrified and thrilled.
Hopelessly nobbled by Nietzsche,
you hobbled past a purblind creature,
reached the Steps—and shook!
Great literature flew from you like doves.
Humbled by such munificence,
I led you back to our hotel
and now, when young colleagues
wish to borrow my *Prime of Life*,
I warn them, 'Mind you bring it back.
It was stolen for me by a great friend.'

I Recognize My Brother in a Dream
for Robert Rose

Run to ground in a desecrated cemetery
by the Murray River, I am told a power failure
has occurred in the town's electricity plant,
throwing the entire region into darkness,
an existential night in which the ubiquitous
love-maddened cicadas and the Jewel Hotel's
sun-wizened inhabitants fall silent for a moment
before droning intoxicatedly on. Immediately
I set off for the library where I work,
to help offload books and reassure chiefs,
the computer no doubt having gone down,
thrown into a sort of crimson chaos. As I go,
rushing down broad avenues of sullen ochre,
avoiding the prams that flash across my path,
my feet send up hurricanes of dust and I glimpse
neurotic women clambering into fetid attics
laden with tawdry hatboxes. Frightened,
I tell myself I am not afraid and resolve
to creep quietly on. On the pavement
oily, parasitical insects insinuate themselves
in sandy rivulets like scorched flesh,
so that, near the town hall, all gothic emanation
and tarnished gargoyle, I find myself longing
for the unspeakable rites of a carrion crow.
Arrived in the main street I weep.
The library, imposingly situated between
the blood bank and the football oval,
is ablaze, everything in it presumably lost:
library staff, manic borrowers, the erudite.
Undismayed, teams of earnest young firemen
compete to douse what yet might prove
superior to flame, unleashing swollen hoses
and flicking them about like nightclub singers
with their microphone cords, so officiously
I no longer misgive. Further along

stands a two-storey block of flats,
ugly, stuccoed, rented, utilitarian,
designed only to withstand the erosion
of a certain stoic architectural standard.
Upstairs three boys are leaning out of
a window festooned with purple ribbons,
jeering at something which I cannot make out.
The youngest is shorter and blonder than
I recall, his face vivid and suntanned
and smiling like that of an angel.
With uncanny attention to detail
and though I am many years his senior,
he describes the furnace for me:
how its flames torment the woodwork,
lifting great sheets of bubbling yellow paint,
and hordes of camera-laden spectators
cringe behind their cordoned safety.
Only then, as in a paradisic dream,
do I recognize my young guide as my brother.

Operamanes

Yet they accuse us of being dilettantes!
A colleague interrupts my matutinal gloom
to announce that his father shared
a first-wicket partnership with mine
thirty-seven years ago during Country Week.
He even recalls the sweep that got you out,
himself scoring a century
to your costive forty-three.
(History might like to reverse this.)
Another year, serving behind the bar
at the Collingwood Social Club,
I listened to a core of die-hards
extol your prodigious torpedo punt
in the 1953 Grand Final,
the rare projectile artistry of it.
One went on to declare that
only a monumental shirtfront
stood between you and the '55 flag.
Anyone else would have sagged on a stretcher,
but not you—so the aria went.
Marvelling at my half-time rhapsodists
I mistook them for a coloratura's claqueurs,
devotees of Callas's phrasing in the
recitative leading up to 'Casta diva',
an erotic thrill in 'Ah fors'è lui'.
We are all of us clamant in the gods,
avid, hyperventilating,
worshipping with stinging hands.

The Wall

The great wall is universal.
The great wall is what you dream about,
Vast and sacred and amorphous.
The great wall is there for all of us to see,
To run our hands over,
To train vines and paint murals.
Graffiti mocks a buttress
And the great wall rides a tremor
Like a blond his seismic wave.
Built by mullocks to withstand attack
She is man's one great insurmountable fact,
Totem-sheer, moon-inane.
All through history they gathered here
To barbecue tough hairy juiceless boars.
They wiped their hands on leaves
Instead of napkins, but they too had
Their flasks and flans and prodigious sleeps.
Pasty-faced women snuck off behind a blackboy
To gossip about this one's ostentatious pav.
The good went for intramural strolls, raving on.
This one set his sights on a raised rock
And found five black snakes sunning themselves.
How he ran and ran through the writhing gorge
Where idiots and mystagogues alike dangled
From trees. There was blossom too,
Pink and cherubic—ditto lovers,
Nature's unreconstituted lambs.
Too-imaginative youths convinced themselves
That a queer sunstreak engendered life.
Others, autodidacts and -erotics,
Lost themselves in Teach Yourself Books
Or Greatest Ever Novels,
Wondering how close they'd come
To leading interesting lives,
Those subliminal drifts through Lambinet.

An elderly couple took a rug,
Some even recklessly made love,
Sprawled beneath the desecrated arch
Where soot was already forming,
The very spot where centuries later
A child would be sacrificed,
Sacrificed and buried beneath
The great wall rank and universal,
The smeared, roseate, immitigable wall.

True Confessions

Unversed in Latin,
incapable of Greek,
Kant for me a clausal blur
never ceasing to haunt,
like mystic Russia
and Lord Elgin's marbles,
I am profoundly ignorant
of Hinduism, and deeply fazed
when the subject of Australian wines
is raised, as it often is
during sophisticated dinners.
Like Candide's hapless spinners
or Hulot in Guermantes
I lack the front.
Asked to spell metempsychosis
I blush; hounded for the right
meteorological term for
a squeamish genus of cloud
(even, absurdly,
what makes the sky blue)
I would doubtless fail
a Mastermind audition.
As for childhood,
it never ceases to amaze that
when Mozart wrote lovesick arias
I was more absorbed
in penile heavens.
I am not Björn Borg,
nor alas was meant to be.

Imagining the Inappropriate

Not exactly difficult after a day
spent outfacing dyslexia, consoling
Brahmans in their shag-piled bunkers,
central heating syruping laments.

Kind of the novelist
to descant in Cornish journals
on Vision in the Flinders Ranges;
sweet of the expatriate
to proffer a triolet;
admirable of the Czech soprano
to bare her Butterfly in Narrabri;
oracular of Oscar to civilize
such a turd-shaped continent;
always hilarious when Tarkovsky
and Truffaut send us their cameos.

But why New South Wales in the first place,
for God's sake?
Why am I writing this in Croydon,
in a city named after
an impotent prime minister?
Why does that median strip over there
commemorate a dead mayor?
Why is it that only our rivers run real?
How do we manage to keep a straight face
under this Ruritanian lace?

Imagine waking in astoundment's land,
the ungazetted paradise,
kingless, ruleless, griefless, anthemless,
whose only currency lurks
at the bottom of a lake
and is therefore unattainable,
where the libraries are our legislatures,

cavatinas our major export,
euphorics firing dogma.

Name me a republic
rousing and ringing
as a coital cry,
whose vivid flora
no colonizing nose
has penetrated.

Morning at Kiama

For David Mackie

They have it to themselves this morning,
the dolphins, the gannets, the fishes,
the sea all changeless, temperate,
tilting slowly like a dreaming lover,
slow motion almost.
Sleek, cobalt, deep, unturbulent,
foamless infinitude without form,
the sea rides on musing on a theme,
whether to don its usual crown,
drown some innocent for breakfast.
(In the harbour
where dolphins shelter and are shot
the cortège slowly passes,
a wreath remembers the Italian fisherman,
dead since Tuesday.)
Overhead, demoralized by dawn
and panicky as pedigrees,
squat clouds rearrange themselves.
A skiff with red sails tacks
across the sun. On the cliff
lies a solitary, domed in exotica.
And the moon, perfect, ovular,
that cheered us last night
as we made our way home,
its journey almost done.

The Wind Debates Asian Immigration

Skipping along the footpath
two Asian brothers chatter
on their way to school,
witty, laden, immaculate,
grinning at the possum
splayed on the bitumen,
entrails cemented
by the morning traffic.
Near the junction both
are startled by a tabloid
smacking in the wind,
vortical riot of opinion
choreographed by idiots.

The Siamese Twin Condition

The French have a saying for it, I'm told.
Pessimistic colleagues
carry it round in their wallets,
next to poems from *The New Yorker*
backed by special offers
on inflatable iguanas.
Empires and emporia tend to
regulate the commoner conditions,
but in the end I can't remember
whether it was two or four years
allotted to us. Whatever it was,
rest assured, we exceeded it.
Now all I know is that
the old viscerations abate,
give way to a kind of Methodist languor,
like going a whole week without a drink.
Ceremonies that once inspired
their own ceremoniousness
pass by unattended.
Our future will not be spent
roaming through landscapes
sepiaed with significance.
When you mention revisiting
a certain part of town,
the quarter of ineluctable attractions,
when you gossip about the clamour and the wine,
looking at me with those lashes
to see how I'll take it,
try though I may I can't react,
I feel nothing, I begin to daydream
about coral, snorkelling, the price of petrol—
I even hear myself hoping
you have a smooth entry.

The Classicist's Birthday Tribute

Beneath the expressionist Judas,
vomiting his brilliant coinage,
two women speculate
about a colleague's tips,
or are they real?

Outgallanting death,
urbane as an elegant fowl,
a bourgeois pushes his wife's
wheelchair, so sweetly
it could be a waltz.

Then a courtly purblind mannerly man,
led by his son. Squinting
at the walls he prefers his own
Entombment to the one on show.
Rather more life, he says.

Fascicles for Emily

1.

I watched a Sunset in my yard —
It lay down by the dam —
Embarrassing a chestnut teal —
Soon fond as lover's arm —

I wondered what the night adduced —
Where conversation led —
What imitations Sun told teal —
What poetry they read —

By dawn the Calm had gendered Strife —
Turmoil ruled — and the Wind —
And opposite — Empurpled day —
The West — bewildering!

2.

Dim Volleys of Catastrophe
Invade the ticking house —
Amaze me into Consciousness —
Unlace the dreaming spouse —

Or was it War of theirs I heard —
A Bomb beside me laid?
Some souls are Little Corporals
On nightly Escapade —

3.

Sometimes the Lear of Tragedy
Seems jovial beside
The faces met on Boulevards—
The Grove of Suicide—

No Parricide of Sophocles
Rehearsed a Woe like this—
Poor Oedipus—his sight restored—
Has supper at the Ritz—

Some lives are mere Appurtenance—
Auditions in the Soul—
More poignant than the Dramatist's
Frenetic curtain-call—

In venues far from Vaudeville
Bank, bakery and booth—
They ply their jeeps with Sufferance—
Confound the Panto's truth—

For Arcades thrive on Gravitas—
And market it as Glee—
A Commerce like the Alchemist's—
Strange Wound like Subtlety—

4.

Saw majesty arraigned last night—
Escorted from the House—
The Gendarme with the lucid whip—
Confecting his Cross—

Yet no one came to save Signor—
Livelong solitary—He—
So furtive was Officialdom—
On lonely Calvary—

5.

Like a Man without a Symptom
I quit the Mortal House—
Behind me lay the Cemetery—
And marbled Eulogist—

What mouths were these that tombed my way?
What cushions in the soil?
What ignorance inspired the mass
To doubt my abstract toil?

6.

I turned a monumental Key—
Quite accidentally—
Releasing all the Innocents—
Like Rocco in a play—

As if enspelled the brute were blithe—
And Sordor splendid day —
Nostalgic is our Tenement
For Freaks of Liberty —

The House of Vitriol

Here it is always St Cecilia's Day.
At night we listen to the same music,
Glibly emoting according as the arrow
Is calm or epileptic.
Sound experts plunder my heart nightly.
From overture to cabaletta
We swan through the Dead City
Then on to Hansel and Gretel,
Drinking metropolitan wines
And nibbling cheese.
Infatuated with improbabilities,
I am as alone as it is possible to be,
In company, though accomplices,
Cowed by so much self-mockery,
Predict a brilliant career in politics.

$\sim$

('It was at the Florentino, was it not, my dear,
That we got our pronouns horribly twisted,
Blushing into our respective soufflés?
Glazed effigies of prime ministers looked on unamused.')

$\sim$

Say you are
Say you are only
Say you

$\sim$

The girl at the door disturbs my dreams,
The more ominous shape at the window
My more erotic tea-breaks.
Both shiver as if they have seen a ghost.

The girl sells chocolates,
He is coatless.

～

When it comes to publishing novels
We leave out Nietzsche.
Others weren't so coy,
Boasting of bestialities.
This one wrote himself into a corner
Signing too many cheques.
Plucked off Kings Cross (reportedly)
Wearing only a fedora. Chic!

～

And the boys' brown eyes bent beneficently
Wink.

～

We all tell the same jokes,
Only some with more panache.
You are the original zealot in overalls,
Transmogrified, resurrected.
Your humour is as black as his,
And merciful.

～

Say you are gone, over
Say you are my mystery and my chaos
My riches and my poverty
My shame and my impenitence
The full frontal metaphysic

All life and no time
Or vice versa

~

We go there sometimes,
Bawling at local residents.
It's hard not to be real on a bicycle
But Datsuns have better acoustics.
Through the slime and the putrescence
We climb up sculpted river banks
Intoning misdirections
While a moulting sky dispenses electric rain
On an unforgiving populace.

~

And the boys' brown eyes bent beneficently

~

In the Doge's Palace everyone's a shepherd.
Renaissance men all have bars on their windows
To protect encyclopedic reputations.
You meet them sometimes,
Going up one-way streets the wrong way

~

Say you are
Say you are only
Say you

~

Now
In the present tense
It is you

Now
In the fecund sense
What once was hers
Which now is yours
And it is you
Now is

('It was at the Florentino, was it not, my dear?')

It is your mock-dwelling I approach
Bringing burnt offerings.
It is your alligator I taunt,
Your blunt instruments I admire.

Your offer to soundproof the recesses of my psyche
Is repulsed with smiles.

Not for you the riddles and epiphany

You are the rope of the city
That coils through my imagination
Slicked back,
Liquefying, putrefying.

You are the infection and the squalor
The charnel house of desire
The vicious simultaneous waltz

No one leads; both follow.
Brassily the band plays the best of Lehár.
You are the umpteenth, inevitable saint.

Your voice on the other end of the phone,
So weak tonight, suggests delirium.
(Are you aware?)

You of the drollest imaginings

My solace and my devastation

In whose arms
We go on vying
All the mad quadrilles of our days and nights

The Catullan Rag (1993)

Aviator

A portrait of him standing there
would be enough now—
easeful and sleek despite
bitters of another year
less cogent than the last,
which he relates,
stroking an agile neck.
Evening on his skin
is subtle and chemical,
furtive as a connoisseur
not yet emboldened, plotting
future carnivals of touch,
but critical, vigilant,
appraising the several strokes
of his casual beauty—
olive skin, alien cross,
teak glint of languid eyes
that appraise, too,
in their franker way,
asking weighted questions:
avocation, destination,
how I like to spend my nights.
A portrait of him standing there
would be enough now.

Parsifal

It was when you told me of the gypsy in your blood
(compound profanish and coursable
in veins I traced through imagination)
that I recognized my possibility
and went to you, silhouetted
in the notorious darkness,
slowly removing the red sock
like the Prelude we had played and played
in the attitude of strangers.

Cactus

Just what the needleman said,
and well worth waiting for—
like love or real tomatoes.
Once every lustrum they ignite,
plosive as Indonesian matches,
amethyst on the sun's wrist.

Noritake

How she must have hated those Saturdays:
the spidery chaos and primitive accounts.
Not that it would have shown as she took
the keys from dowagers with arms that shook.
Burgher and indigent she treated the same,
each puerile oddment wrapped like a jewel.
Charity she understood perfectly,
with an instinctive altruism I had to simulate,
catching myself in the counter glass.
What baffled was the lure of squalor,
rusty grace of second-hand toasters,
chipped Noritake polluted and pre-lipped.
Meant to keep her company,
I preferred the recesses of the Op Shop,
galleries of wardrobes and prototypical televisions.
There I could rave to myself, elaborating narratives
I wove each summer—epics of Monopoly,
the most divorced prime minister in history!
This was my stoa, my pantheon,
a Reading Room of poseurs in preposterous suits,
One day, dislodging a stack of *Weeklys* and Plaidys,
I found a mint copy of Garnett's life of Lawrence,
recognizably rare. Next Monday,
speech rehearsed, I showed it to the master
who had introduced me to Lawrence,
was pleased when he borrowed it.
A fortnight later came the limp, bibliophilic excuse—
a summer storm, the cover ruined, our mystery dashed.
To compensate, he gave me a copy of Palinurus,
adjuring me to read six marked passages
'and any five other pages'. I was fourteen.
Years later, resigned to the treason of elders,
I follow his red instructions, turn to

de Quincey on marriage: 'so exquisite
a traffic of selfishness that it could not yield
so much as a phantom model of society.'

The Living Archive
for my mother

Unwrapping a pair of luxurious towels—
one so dark as to be almost black,
the salesman quipped, stroking it
and his permanent wave, marvelling
at my tangible cash, the other
vaguely ruby for an anniversary—
unfolding these and holding up the
marked-down clock bought that morning
in a jeweller's shop half sealed-off,
as if pearl and choker no longer paid,
you answered our facetious question
rather earnestly, which was unexpected,
saying you couldn't recollect unmarried life,
the twenty-odd years romanticized by a
fantastical son: waitress, stenographer,
the stoic girl outbraving rheumatic fever
(not once complaining, an uncle said),
one of Mario's dark-haired croonettes,
advised to concentrate on opera by a
visiting Italian tenor, but already
contracted to a bantamweight from the bush,
I have files on you and fingerprints
and photographs, yet the shards of memory
disintegrate under out feet—
leave me sentimental and otiose,
Antonia's archivist in the Offenbach,
the last romantic to convert to disc.
By then it was time for a toast,
my father and brother with their sudsy beer,
the two of us sipping nostalgic sherry,
as if the decades hadn't materialized
and a different dog wriggled on the rug.
Later, at the restaurant, for entrée
you served up familial anecdotage
(not your traditional fare): tales of

Robert's lethal cocktail, tripping
over snakes in the Warby Ranges,
our first morning in Auckland
when a bus missed my by that much.
If I knew this I had forgotten.
And what to do with a two-year-old's
first foreign foolhardiness,
often re-enacted on conscious kerbs?
Then the joke was on the guests,
all our respective anniversaries.
Around the table we went in a divorcing wave,
none outlustring the unimaginable ruby.
Like Donne's computing lovers
I stall at the first and vainly project.
Chuckling at his end of the table,
the best my brother could do was three,
which we christened the Tinfoil Anniversary.

Polyphony

No, this is not exactly silence,
hovering like a stentor menace,
the one not countenanced in years.
Opposite, an oily Dimplex sloshes
to itself, timing our anxieties.
Tacit, a string quartet
elbows in the corked void,
bowless Bartók listenable only
in suave, improbable states.
Lath, pillar and rafter creak,
then the demotic buzz of electricity,
a refrigerator changing key,
ushering its signature tune.
Downstairs, valetudinarian lungs
braid the chronic past. Nosing,
the methodical gut pursues
its dark destiny. Somewhere,
a last train, a young man
unchaining his bicycle. Whistling,
a neighbour spills his gourd of keys.
Still strangers after years,
we nod across the mural dark.
Sneezing with fright, a possum
arcs from a corrugated roof.
Something switches itself off.
And always, just a hand, a flame,
the loquacious prompt of the brain:
tedious, bitter, extravagant,
if not morose and sentimental,
that will be acknowledged
like a diva. Not exactly silence.

Podvig

for Louise Sweetland

In one of Nabokov's early novels
(Russian mazes seemingly composed
for witty prefacing in the cloudage
of Montreux) the widowed Sofia,
endowed with one of those stigmata
captured only by Vladimir's humane lens —
pale slits left by absent earrings
hocked for a counter-revolution
or to mend a shoe — interrupts
her lament about famine and
the Bolsheviks to declare,
'Look isn't that cliff
beautifully lit up over there?'
Abruptly I am reminded of a colleague
whose birthday it was today.
'Forty-four and I can't bear it,'
she moaned, doomful with sarcasm,
her life nearly over. So I went out
and bought a cake at the Europa,
and we all crammed into her office
wheeling ergonomic chairs,
some bearing all-purpose cards kept
for eleventh hours in a bottom drawer.
'Happy margins,' they scribbled
in their irreverent, primary hands.
Instead of hangovers and romantic fissures
everyone wanted to discuss the crisis
in the Gulf, last night's bodings
on the televised panel,
a run on gas masks in Geelong.
Remembering something carnal in a dream,
I heard you say sotto voce,
'I can't help thinking
about all their mothers.'
You had a son yourself quite late.

Three and a half, he rings you up
like a nagging author, your own
magnum opus with the reckless royalty.
If only it came down to this
in the deserts and the chambers,
the studios and the mortuaries:
a belated mother's appalled sanity.
But does not—and later,
when we had all gone, back to
our galleys and out blueprints,
you shrieked at me from the next room,
'Quick—hurry—look at the rain.
It's marvellous. So straight.
We could be in Singapore.'

Carpenter's Cup

Like a retributive elder
he shows up once a year
to spike a tap or bruit a hole.
Only my cracked landlord
would pay him to spatter
lino, confound a hinge.
Chaos his intimate angel,
he whistles three dirgeful notes,
audible for several blocks.
Longing to shut him up
I'm asked for my tip in the Cop
and why I'm not listening.
Like me, he went once,
forty years ago,
just back from the war.
Not that he lost much—
merely wasted a day:
the ladies in their silk,
the steeples of conversation,
the pointless, invisible geldings.
He never went back.
Not to Caulfield or Flemington,
Not to the new tracks
ringing the sovereign stakes.
'Better to stay home
and make something.'
Better to drive the tenants
mad with a dissonance
of dirgeful notes.
Again I heft the bathroom door.
Again the hinge is misaligned.
Curses follow, and a slimy tea.
Resigned to tedium
of anecdote and afternoon,
I settle on the sofa,

fashioning a finish
condign to the times.
Reaching for Scholes's *Companion*
I study a Batt engraving:
the Introspective Schumann,
who spent his afternoons
in the Leipzig Kaffeebaum,
always staring at the wall,
mouth open as he whistled,
'softly and to himself'.
My carpenter would understand
the solace of a yieldless wall,
how the banalest chord,
played often enough,
somehow codifies life,
flat, lento, isolate.

Googly

Shadowed by a divvy van,
thirty punks annex a park,
blue heelers zigzag for
ice cream and cupped Fanta.
Wheeling round, an auctioneer
is dispossessed, neglects a bid.
Flamingo forearms semaphore
a sky ribbed with tattoos.
Night visitants wear black,
chained leather a punic shell.
Runt Ariels pogo under saffron hair.
Grubbing for entertainment,
they pluck stakes for stumps
and compose elevens. The sweeps
are raw, vigorous, though girls
in weeds make sportive umpires,
run out the stoned, the anarchic.

Vantage

Hanging out the stained tablecloth
and several monogrammed handkerchiefs
that once belonged to my father, I look up.
It is a high wild imperious handsome day.
I had it to myself for an hour
like an ambivalent character in Conrad,
nautical man alone with his dyspathy.
Now, looking round me, I confront
a universe like an empirical zoo,
everyone watching: a stunned young man
washing up in his hungover way,
a calico cat wedged in its tree
patient for doves, that elderly
Russian woman leaning from her window,
drying her grey magisterial hair.
Staring, just starting, everybody staring.
Or is this egoism, morning's fine way
of mocking an unshaved transcendentalist?
Today I feel like greeting each of them singly,
Charlestoning across this concrete courtyard,
essaying some ludicrous summery gesture—
though when I venture 'Good morning'
the Russian woman goes on staring,
her mannish mouth ambiguously grave.
Conceivably deaf, incontestably beautiful,
this was someone's Beatrice,
leaning now from her window in a suburb
thousands of miles from the known
and the ardent. What is it you would
have me say? she insinuates,
unravelling her grey magisterial hair
while I stroke the belled calico cat,
admire the republic of verdure canopying
our shared courtyard. Last night
it was a refuge for insolent possums,

maddening my neighbour's Airedale,
forcing an early waking—not unwelcome.
Again I greet my ironic Russian,
sternest of sharers. Again, no answer.
Yes, it is a high wild imperious handsome day.
Upstairs my espresso pot has long boiled dry,
the companionable stock flavours the flat
with rosemary and celery and thyme.
In a blind room at the end of the hall
a tender guest, laziest of celebrants,
wakens in my bed, traces the knots
and fjords of my absence. Calling.

Compact Disc

It's probably always like this,
the evening wearing on, wearing out,
inflamed like a sky lit
for a coronation, a sesquicentenary,
brusquely quelled like Dulcamara's diagnosis:
'Burnt lips, fudged arteries, skew breast'—
Renaissance theories about
the tilt of the globe.
Moments before you arrive,
scrupulously late,
the radio announcer,
betrayed by his own *Heldentenor*,
announces Jussi Björling
and Zinka Milanov's recording
of the Act One duet from *Tosca*.
Drunk on sound and mad gulps of pernod
I play it very loud,
play it even louder when you arrive.
Hesitant, half-hearted, mismatched,
about to inaugurate
our ninth life together,
we stand in the hallway
shouting clichés at each other.

Metro

And there was no one else in the park that night,
the long one snaking through the bourgeoisie
down which you led me endlessly,
chilled to the bone,
with a kind of viral foreboding.
Why should there be anyway?
Whom would you expect at this hour of night,
the map of the world curing a rattle?
Give me one tall notable reason.
the sort of upstart found in Joshua Reynolds.
Call it cogent. Pile it on like impasto,
rashly lampooned in the underground,
such is our poverished vanitas.
Where else does it lead
but the Café Eurydice,
not a good place to get lost, I say.
Imagine him driving away
with a bull terrier named Clarence
and you have the real wrong picture.
Fancy him sinuous and white-bodied,
calling for the reckoning.

Dog Days
for Gwen Harwood

After the blazoned festival,
the luminous photography,
the row of intelligent banners,
Chinese lanterns glowing
in their plane trees;
after the committees,
the televised rehearsal,
the tense unbibulous launch,
one window open only
on a city impossibly far:
it is with more that relief
that I walk an aged beagle,
my unliterary but truly
civilized friend, who
tolerates out sentimental
one-sided conversation,
veering on aromatic detours,
tugging at the dewy grass
like a class traitor.
Enervation too accompanies me,
pulling on its choker collar—
dogging me like a mal de flanc.
Hungry, needful in my own way,
I memorize the faces of joggers
and strollers, young men
with first gingery moustaches,
tweaked by impertinent sisters;
marvel at the multiplicity of
children, the kaleidoscope
of human hair, lank, curly,
titian, punk-onyx. Only
an Indian boy, pigeon chest
pursing with fright, resists
the flirting of an aged beagle.
Then a phrase moving through

my heart, through my blood,
like one last slow rapture.
The exquisite Indians.
How it struck us simultaneously
as we sat in that bar years ago,
drinking beer after our crazy
cycle round the island.
The exquisite Indians.
Incantation of envy almost.
Around us belched and swaggered
Cowes's boozy youth, commercial
T-shirts bulging and stained.
No silk here. One glance
and you left our window perch,
joined the couple posing their
grinning black-eyed children
against a war memorial,
offered to frame them,
clasped and bewildered,
against a vast immartial sea,
came bounding, buoyantly, back,
as if we could shed racial inanity
for a moment in that disco bar.
Now I am far from ocean,
far from strait, long separated
from that known blue whelm.
Gathering night will not ferry me
to some convivial harbour
for wine and fish and company.
It is retreat that I seek
in my urban, secular way,
following a concrete path
sorrelled for municipal tastes.
Around me, like a lethargic chorus
slow to assemble, a bar

too late for 'Va, pensiero',
unfurls the missioned blossom,
nature's sold-out epiphany.
Now only the budless witch-elm
drags its heels, gothic, misshapen
amid spring's muscular shield.
Like an extra, I move through
groves of wattle fiery as
sharp pain, a beautiful migraine.
Disentangling olfactory dogs
I skirt the grey-haired woman
in their tonish slacks,
give way to electric daughters
executing their power walk,
that absurdest strut in history.
But I'm not even watching
or listening. The opera is over,
the point made and the Hebrews
gone home. Before I know it
I've reached the eucalypt
where I always turn—I'm not
sure why: habit, superstition,
predictable as a panting jogger
consulting his wrist, above all
sentimental about nature,
even on this tenuous reserve
five minutes from a freeway.
But I'm not even drifting,
lost in a welled atavistic sleep
to renege on life. I remember
reaching this outermost gum,
bluish bourne of the known,
in a similar trance, bleak,
catatonic, chain-smoking
underneath it for an answer,

so intent on solitude
I rued the human dot slowly
dilating on the horizon.
Today it is an old beagle
waddling towards me,
discreet, wary, just smiling,
like a timid man visiting
a mentor of whom he's unsure—
victim of some wilful malady.
So I frisk her ears, dance about,
declaim poems she fails to hear.
Now I'm like a West Highland
terrier let off its chain,
indulging in a moment's
boundless, futuristic dynamism—
except I long in my own way
for the faint impress of the collar,
the slow bruise of the familiar,
the sharp tug on the gnostic leash.

The Only Farewell

Now it flowered on you like coral
of a coruscating kind
and I moved towards you
in a trace of pulleys,
knowing this would be the only farewell,
twining expiation on expiation,
as memory, flawed and tuneful memory,
shivered across me like
the voluptuary's most painterly cloud.

Confetti

Like opposing hemispheres of the brain:
the city on the one hand,
mercantile and pendulous,
a row of royal chequers
swept by scienced clerks—
that sleek river on the other,
surging like a numinous vein
on a beautiful hand, perfecting
the withdrawn hand as a jewel,
black and exceptional,
adorns mere animated bone.
Imagination welling in its mac,
you talked of going skating
on this frigidated vein,
talked of taking someone
you were in love with, though
it seemed doubtful as the weather
as we drove and drove,
quite hard in retrospect
and fearlessly, trying to make sense
of the scattered shapes
in the chronic squall,
trying to humour it with the
dullest Broadway lyric imaginable,
not hard after the confessional reading,
the brutish wine, the audience of nine.
So we skidded on an oily catwalk
where confetti once lodged
in a filmed eye and she wept
throughout the long dutiful ceremony,
What it is we strive for
in the clutch of out self-harness:
hot chocolate, the diarist's
nibbling foreplay, a new nape
to tongue and tongue?

Well, I dwell on the left side
of the brain, past the river,
in the neighbourhood of dust and drab
and granulated crime, where roads
flaunt the atrocious fig and
young men in black political leather
glace and glide along the railway track.

The Best of Fleetwood Mac

The gulf between a mute, elementary
kitchen and the more garrulous
maisonette is so mandatory,
so legalistic, as to entice only choirs
of staring cats and matted kittens,
broodily attuned to dementia of plumbing,
like wizards of the waiting-room.
Across this torpid lantern-jawed strip
down which randy beams tilt
when you least expect,
the Best of Fleetwood Mac
winds down on its crusted track,
convulses like an urban journey,
as if some grave, dilating guitarist,
the Seneca of Woodstock, digits
and features crippled in surprise,
reckons with the Parousia of Marketing.
Now only the uxorious pigeon's
captious insight rides the novel air,
affronting limb-locked plane trees;
and a transcendental Spitfire
bombarding our sluttish suburb
with sachets of pink detergent.
But this is another century,
another kind of phoney war,
the politicians' noses powdered
on one side like fruity overtures.
When at last I am free to begin,
when I plug these dubious imaginings,
I find I have no appetite for laundry
or marauding — not as free as I thought.
What shall I do with this thing, this life?
Where shall I bury it, dragging
a recusant spine over terminal ice?
In the bright mauve curtainless cell

opposite mine, confronting it even
like a glib date capable of one lisped taunt,
a precocious Jewish boy, on holidays
from California, lambasts his adoring aunts,
listing all their moral deficiencies:
trite coffee, falsetto chat,
fond talk at midnight through a wall.
Now and then, exploding their shy defences
like the brilliant attorneys he aspires
to be, he consults my herby sill,
sane jury of thyme and fennel and marjoram,
to watch them batten on his rhetoric.

A Succession of Suns

Anyway, that's roughly how it started,
the chronology a little stagnant,
beyond mere clockwork, mere speculation
about human nature, how it runs down
like sympathy in the stalls.
What's left is the inartistry of cameras
over your left shoulder,
temerities of tourists quelled
by the frogs' lilied anthem,
all the poets scheming in the chapel.
What is it this time but fiscal etiquette
and the comity of slums?
So you wait for the diffident man
to phone about his blue container,
the one with all the capped answers.
Hired to interrogate angels, oracles,
to capture an enigmatic voice
as it breaks, he is rapt conjecture
and the scars of a thousand conditions.
Meanwhile civilization happens
in its crypts and cafés,
oases of verse for which no one can supply
the appropriate half-rhyme. Giacometti
could do something with this elongation,
you there sprawled on the rocks,
prodigal and carnified, lately
restored to your quondam element,
the palaeontologist's amorous fossil.
Sunburst now is a spasm of bathos
despite vigils of destitute morning,
the clumsy verses in the bay window.
Yesterday it hung there,
abstract, suspenseful,
like angular beauty surprised
in its everyday mirror.

I though of all the regulated dazzle
waiting to happen without you,
the seasons of water lilies
and reveries of strawberries,
all the languid, memoried afternoons,
duettists making their way dumbly,
solicitously, through the historic garden.
All our constitutionals take us past
altitudes and platitudes where
something was ventured once in a
different posture, as if this world
of ceaseless intersecting traffic
is a ritual of inefficient angels,
the two of us intimate, opposite,
shored inside the same language.

Ornithology

Fazed by a corps of gulls
never seen before—
squat warriors with gourmet beaks
and brilliant, jagged helmets—
I turn to you, already framing
my old embarrassed question:
What bird is that?
But the beach is long and echoless,
stirred only by scrums of seaweed,
a lone trepid blond on his wave,
bits of shell the gull tore from the crab.
Where is my ornithologist now?
Where is mastery when I need it most?
Only the new tide greets me,
put its arms round me, leads me
onto the glistening dance floor.

Bait

It was one of your last visits.
My memory is sharp, even clinical,
gives interviews like a criminal.
After the exchange of looks,
the tentative opus of Beethoven,
I asked you to help me lay
prophylactic baits in the ceiling,
famous phobic that I am.
'Pent up in lath and plaster'
like Melville's urban sentinel,
separated by more than cornicing,
by a furlong of insular feet,
I followed you from room to room,
listened to you crawling overhead,
diligent, hawking, asthmatic,
grazing your head on a beam.
After a moment's unexplained dream
(were you brooding or baiting or both?)
you came down ashen and loath —
time for a mithridatic kiss.
Now it seems final and fitting
as all the other rituals:
the oblivion of Scotch,
the loving calumnies of friends,
a fortnight's interminable diarising
while an unseasonable blizzard
wrapped Padua in white.

Wart

So now it's your turn
to flourish in Tuscany,
reel drunkenly round Bernini's
spinning colonnade, gnomic
as Berenson conquering the Pitti.
While you languish in Perugia,
wondering which piazza
deserves your midnight patronage,
I celebrate in my own way,
cutting a Grolier edition
of *Romeo and Juliet* proffered
years ago on my own return.
The sole gift that day was yours—
awkward invert of romance.
But why am I so obsessed
by how much you paid for it?
Why do I borrow a magnifying glass
to stymie your diligent erasure?
Sadly revealed, the inflated price
takes my breath away. Relaxing the glass,
I spot my first new wart in years.

'The Catullan Rag'
(1986–2004)

KITCHEN

Lesbia, Lesbia, look at me now.
Stop fretting tomorrow night's *boeuf*.
It's only cow! I want to feel those
frantic arms around me, the sun
catching their short blonde hairs just so.
Can't we lose ourselves for a moment?
Can't we wallow and accept,
alone, unmade, like a maniac's bed?
The pores on your face have never
been so exposed. Like myriad
tired eyes they stare at me. So!
Let this sallow flesh sag together.
No one will notice. No one will care.
The world is a prentice decades
our junior, ardent, callow, merciless,
forever cutting his teeth. So come now,
right here, amid the refuse,
amid the bottles and detritus.
Let us consummate what the times portend.
The squalor is playing our song.

SCARF

What provoked it, Lesbia—
bells ringing as you woke,
fanatically hungover,
with a foul taste in your mouth?
Did you break that old rule of yours,
the one that's served you so well,
about never going back, never watching
an express pull out of the station?
Did you splash on some tropical scent,
recover the silk scarf immortalized
in a dozen novellas, veteran
of more dinners than the Begum Khan?
Did you kill two birds with one stone,
as they say (though not you, Lesbia),
interrupting the gallery crawl,
the amused post mortem of our Italian waiter,
who remembered you, I have no doubt,
and stood up a little hurriedly,
righting a chair? Did you clear your throat,
accept your first cigarette of the day,
a glass of Amaretto? Did you ask?
Did you ask about our table, Lesbia—
any other discards found in that
tight little corner near the door?

SUNDAY PROFILE

Artist, savant, intellectual—
to me you're none of these,
despite your flip modesty
in the colour magazines,
triple-chinned on Lygon Street,
pinkly hairless in jacuzzis.
'For breakfast, grams of muesli
and elective garlic tablets.
Willingly he forgives those
who reject him: the women,
the dachshunds, the children.
Nowadays, for relaxation,
early Waugh and Spielberg movies.'
Tell them about your mornings then—
won't you let the cameras there?
I'd make the cadet reporter
appreciate your richer artistry.
Tea-addict. Nose-picker.
Weathercock. Masturbator.

GLOVES

Squeezing into Catullus's farty Fiat,
Thallus demands a lift to his Carlton midden,
the squat he shares with chemical Muses.
Easing his subsidised arse onto the seat
he pockets a pair of glamorous gloves
left on the dashboard, kid from the gods.
It's so brazen he must want Catullus to freak.
Catullus, used to kleptomaniacs, says nothing,
but that night it goes into the avenging journal
and before too long it's doing the rounds
of caustic dinner parties, seasoning
Catullus's monologue like a toxic herb.
What were you thinking of, Thallus?
Are your hands so cold from all that onanism?
Keep the gloves: press them against your pocked cheek.
That's the closest you'll come to charitable Catullus,

RENASCENCE

And why is Catullus so pleased
with himself this morning,
swaggering round the market
though we know very well his cupboard
is full of firm ripe vegetables?
Whence came this new insouciant Catullus,
this panther of the boulevards,
so athletic and witty and buoyant?
Which fond god fired a second sun
to tan him to such perfection,
compelling married women to look
at him sideways, the devastated roué
to grip him baldly on the street
and ask if he's turned sixteen yet
(Catullus, who has survived
thirty campaigns in love's theatre)?
Could it have something to do
with Catullus's new haircut,
the stray boyish sideburned look?
Or was it that dream last night,
the one he shares glibly
with stranger and old foe,
such is his new magnanimity:
hovering above the campagna
like Giotto's human curtain-rail,
flirting with handsomer peasants
naked and glistening over their ploughs?
Or is this gusto merely dermatological:
the death of eczema! no more nights
torridly masturbating lobe, knuckle
and scalp? You want the truth?—
well, it's none of these.
If everything Catullus says

is memorable, if he seems to gain
eight inches overnight, if the smile
dazzling vatic and virgin
irradiates him even in sleep,
it's because Lesbia has just boarded a jet
bound for the Maldives—and Catullus
is ransomed, whole again, utterly free.

WUNDERKIND

Musing over port
Socration styles himself
our leading young poet
and scoffs at the notion
of lyrical ladies.
Women are there
to edify and squeeze.
But given his thinning hair
and widow's stoop,
the Festschrift subsidised
from his own salary,
it's an antique fiction.

LITIGANT

Socration loves to litigate
as much as he needs to fellate.
He's always limping off to his lawyers,
as he likes to call them.
Cranky Caesar has nothing on him.
Merely hint that Socration
was married to the hapless Olivia
or fathered a soccer-loving lad
and he'll sue you in a trice.
'We were never close,'
he swears in an affidavit.
As for his parents: 'merely acquaintances'.
In public, though, he is serene
and quite beyond defamation.
Give him a platform,
an impressionable audience,
and he is innocent of all the statutes.
All he wants to do
is rhapsodise about Orpheus.

ARCHIVE

Lesbia, tell me it's not true what they're saying
in the brothels and the taverns.
Swear that you haven't sold my letters,
one missive in particular,
to the highest and lowest bidder.
Reassure your morbid love that you
haven't parted with all that's left of him
just to keep your new stud in cock-rings.
(Does he keep you happy, Lesbia?
Where do you go for conversation?
Why don't you twist me instead?
I won't bankrupt you. I don't infect.)
When my friends express alarm,
when loyal-hearted Calvus confronts you,
you insist the file's been marked 'closed',
not to be fingered for a thousand years.
Don't give me that crap, Lesbia.
You're not gurgling to him now, your cockroach.
As if a frilly embargo would stop
all those white-gloved perverts
from salivating over my rank ardour,
dog-earing each foolish, burning page.
Get them back pronto, Lesbia, all of them,
before the facsimiles hit the market
and the baths resound with my aching love,
fit only for music of the karaoke kind.
But tell me there's no truth in it, Lesbia.
Swear it's just another lie, what they're saying
in the brothels and the taverns.

TRUFFLES

Faxing his transparent review
to the *Sunday Void*,
chubby Suffenus regrets
the pleasures of the dining table—
how there'll be no more truffles,
no more vinous introductions
from amiable Catullus.
Maybe not, foxy freelance.
But Catullus is magnanimous,
sends you flagons
of black-label cough mixture.

GLASS

Calvus, this time you have gone too far.
No sophistry will save you now,
no compliment, no hill of figs.
To you I am as cold as a slack lyric,
the sickest emanation of Suffenus
(whose company you share now, be warned!).
Don't be deceived by your consoling henchmen,
those old women who wipe your tears
and pretend it was something you said—
your ludicrous praise for a certain poet
or endless defence of the whimsies of Caesar.
Admittedly, we'd all begun to fade by
the time you reached your verbal peak:
the odyssey of where you found the pork.
But it wasn't that. If for nothing else
I have loved your industrious tongue.
No, the thing that finally did it
was your leaving my glass empty
for forty minutes. Yes, forty—
longer than your epic speeches,
those interminable film plots and dreams.
Perversely you ignored my savage looks,
the glass getting longer, my throat more parched.
Listening to you rave on about your
lost beauty, your burdensome days
all I wanted to do was flee, lose myself
in the liquid company of strangers,
then bugger you in these unforgiving verses.

TERRACOTTA

Typical. You ring up to discuss—
not the hour of your flight nor the length
of your stay in that other country
(land of pale plutocrats and impeccable clocks)—
but a coyly erotic terracotta
you need to stash somewhere.
We were never good at earnests of the real.
That's the last time you'll wake me
for—what?—centuries, months,
the last time the phone will electrify
with your cool and honeyed voice.
Dumb and useless it sits there,
like a vapid guest, a tumorous throat.
If it doesn't ring for a thousand years
I won't be sad. Why not be rid of it,
Catullus—abandon all this cold gadgetry?
Hide it, smash it, tear it from the wall.

Who's Who

There's no getting away from it.
Socration's finally cracked it.
And doesn't he let us know
with his copious press releases.
All night they spew out
maddening the non-elect.
The editors can't have known
what they were doing
when they tapped Socration.
It's the longest entry since
that general who lost the war.
On and on it goes:
every short list he's graced,
every committee harried,
every article inflicted
on the undeserving public.
Why, he even lists the colour of his eyes.
It changes annually, like his title.

TALLY

Lesbia, Lesbia,
I've just been counting
all those poems you fired
that dry month when
we both got thrush
and you went away.
How many would you say?
Try fourteen, and not all bad,
despite your braying
about lurid prolificity.
Send me snaps of your
nostrils flared! Lesbia,
salty never saccharine Lesbia,
percussive as a fatal cocktail
crusting on my lips—
you should leave me more often.

CUT

Oh Suffenus, I knew what
a terrible mistake you were making.
Only you would send back
a dish at the Forum Hotel.
Had I been closer I would have
warned you about the chef's reputation,
but it was such a long table.
Very smug you looked too,
lambasting the waiter in front
of your juicy boys,
insisting that unless they
found a plumper steak
you'd take your party elsewhere.
Applause, applause.
Minutes later, going out for a leak,
Catullus happened to pass the kitchen,
saw the notorious Greek smear it
on his cruel crooked uncut cock—
both sides, abusively—
before returning it to the plate.
How I gagged as I watched you
devour the old meat, boasting
of the fright you'd given them,
of your culinary reputation,
a glob of steak fat on your chin.

CUSTOMS

Lesbia, have you landed?

Unconsciously
I place two bowls
instead of one.

Are you biding by the sea
in a charmless rented weatherboard?

Do you leave the door open at night
for a breeze or strangeness?

What brand do you smoke?
Whose lap cushions your feet
as you read those L.A. novels?

Was that you in my dream,
hauled up a hill,
hieratic and lame?

Lesbia, have you landed?

COLOPHON

Lesbia, beside my bed
are six rare editions from that time.
Precious, they belonged to you
with inscriptions varying
in length, tenderness.
Should I give them back?
Let the auditors remonstrate.
Each colophon was earned.

CINÉMATHÈQUE

Was that you in the dark, Lesbia,
old passion, remembered darling
and burr in my throat? Surely
it was you three rows ahead,
away from the witless gobblers
with noisy cones and baby gossip
(which you silenced with a hiss).
Engrossed though I was
in that old French movie,
the one we'd seen so many times,
now pink with antiquity,
I couldn't help noticing
your outline in the dark,
posture rarely seen in a cinema,
Valhalla to invertebrates.
Where had I known it before?
Then an image of you around dawn
seated at the end of our bed,
your back to me, expectant.
Tonight like an absorbed queen
you sat there unmoving,
not responding to the old nuances,
the killing moment of realisation,
but lighting each subtitle
with your lunar gaze, erect
as Catullus's deathless need for you.

Donatello in Wangaratta (1998)

Greening

Let's not watch the main event,
let's watch the people.
There we shall be beautifully private,
each lake with its own suicide,
those grand disclosures
aching on a beach.
Your beauty is the last quotation,
an available dark.
In the forest, single lights flicker,
day rapturously evokes night.
Soon we shall descend
into the public acre,
a rhapsodist will forfeit
his throne by the view.
So let's postpone matter for a while:
the ritual caper, an auspicious turn.

Shaft

Long, long
like polished stealth
stairs unwind themselves,
prospects on mortality.
Height's not knowing,
nor eventuation,
but chronic flight,
encores of semblances.
Keys in our palm
twitter like biography.
Reckless we begin
to climb, dreading
the final storey,
blatant as a doorway,
virtual as vacancy.
The stairs are strewn
with veiny petals,
ruins of a plenitude.
You have been this way
and I am following.

Steam

What is that strange hoot
ticking horizons,
contorting a neck?
Is it a boy pacing himself,
lone and regular as the day?
Have they reintroduced steam
without alerting the populace,
placing advertisements?

Through the spires
and the lonely chimneys
drift a straggly quotation
and the flags of music.

White Telephone
after Cavafy

How things have changed for him,
if only he cared to historicize.
Exactly two years ago—unimaginable.
It was the phase he had been
dreading, the void between
Christmas and the New Year.
Not once did he go out,
each pointless room in darkness.
All he could do was sit by the
telephone waiting for it to ring,
hating himself, hating the cause,
surrendering to queasy longing.
Stupid: he knew how it must end,
but sat there, fretting a cord.

Now the last thing he craves
is interruption, niceties
of the telephone. Sometimes
he lets it ring, lazy, indifferent.
Yet when he does stir reluctantly
to answer it, he is rewarded—
not so much by the polite,
predictable dinner invitation —
but by the sight of a handsome
young man dawdling beneath
his flat, smoking a last cigarette,
as if remembering someone
sacrificed in a previous city.

Cut-throat

Never more than punctual, I arrive at 9 a.m.,
hair lank from duty's shower, a choice of phrases
to be turned in the chair like monthly civilities:
the state of my business, never named,
soon forgotten; your aged father on Lefkadis.
(That's near Corfu, I'll say. I almost stayed there once
on my way to Brindisi. What's the population?)
We have done this for untold years, a hundred personations.
Some vogues must never grey. This morning, though,
I have been usurped. Bashful and lathered,
the last of your robust sons sprawls in the chair,
tied for the midday interview. Passing the shop,
everyone wishes him luck: florist, beautician,
the angel of cappuccino. Andreas his name is—
tall, handsome, blushful. So father shaves the scion,
barber smooths the tyro, razing a copious beard.
Later, in the same chair, the shop curiously tense,
cologned, I find myself asking about your aged father.
(Which son is that shaving your father on Lefkadis—
all of fifteen?) The answers are always known,
like the drift of a cow-lick. Behind us, mirrored
in a thousand shampoos, beneath the photographs
of desolate models, burdened by switches,
your eldest son and partner shapes the interviewee's locks,
drapes a powerful hand around the fraternal shoulder,
just as his father, dropping his scissors a second time,
lingers on mine for a moment, dreaming of youth
on Lefkadis, the father now eighty-eight—
all the blues of Vassilikis betrayed in a postcard.

Donatello in Wangaratta

It is a kind of speculative night,
the room so close and populous,
resonant with every rover in the town.
A butcher who is all Adam's apple
stammers for a joke. There's talk of
stratagems and cakewalks; some triumph
is intended or delayed. Dumb,
I wake from a terrible gulping sleep,
dreams of an antic pogrom,
the goanna we hacked that afternoon
and threw beheaded in a box.
How we gathered in the dream and in the life—
a posse of us, myself as scout,
surprising it dozing on a fence;
my father, too, awoken from untimely sleep,
singleted in the afternoon, but dutiful.
Then we all looked up and saw,
saw goanna flinching on a wall,
beautiful as the tattooed Icarus
with his methodical axe.
Then sleep, sleep for sleep's sake,
a chant of wasps around a bush
and something leaking in its blood.
Returned blinking to that room
I choose the bonhomie of women,
shades of Swan Street circling
in a sugary alliance. One
I recognize is bearing meringues,
spectacular in their dollopery,
hanging like perilous, illustrated towers.
It must be night, or something obscurer,
ill-defined, say five o'clock,
the light beginning to wane
and something toppling in the fire.
Whose bored hand on the pianola,

strumming not ivory but case?
Whose handsome wrist drawing me
to the isolating performance?
Impatient of music, the pedal of tactics,
childlike despite yourself,
despite your height, your dark evidence,
you finger my new red Caxton encyclopedia,
perplexed at such a gift (for I am six),
turn the page, a robe on enlightenment,
reveal David gleaming, audacious,
uniting us in his slim mimicry.
And suddenly the room is alight,
fired with its own brazen iconography,
silencing and separating as it unites—
hieroglyphics of blood,
sprays of instinct on a wall—
reshaped in its own tense and furtive imagery.

Fog over Corsano

Like auguries the shoals of fog
drift across the slopes of Corsano,
mounting wispy assaults on La Crete.
The vines in the supposed valley
are mere fragrance and birdsong.
Stupid Dominican hounds bark
as they will churl at any weather,
never knowing when to stop,
what started these panics of alarm.
Sight dissolves in a white republic,
the outlines of bodied slopes
frosted with light, delicate, macabre.
Fog has it to itself except for me,
never so alone, domed in solitude.
Faintly a medieval tractor
topples over the clay sculptures,
freshly churned and rife with wheat.
In the distance a solitary cypress
composes itself in the shifting fog,
addresses me like a shadowy flare.
Morning done with flesh,
silhouettes perfect our mortality,
stranding us in a blind ballet.
The tendentious moon, our only effect,
performs its airy dissolution.

James Merrill

Over breakfast I read of your death,
slickest of coronaries, wholly unexpected.
Almost impressive, these spasms of nullity.
How death populates its text. One imagines
your half-smile, a dignified ache —
not the annunciating angel with
votives of discomfiture. Tonight's
poetry reading seems ludicrous,
yet no one rings about a quorum.
We are all cancelled in the end.
Events fiddle with the order,
poison our self-deprecating jokes.
Day that girdled me, laced me with
responsibility, seems futile, anarchic.
Your going like that leaves nothing
to declare, the pattern bogus, azure a blur.
Folding the newspaper, I scan
the street for consequence, watch
Jewish students gathering on a footpath,
pristine for the first day of school.
When the last and tallest of them arrives
he moves through the pack gently
shaking hands. This could be a funeral —
formal giants in their shorts, half-bowing,
commiserative. Then the bus collects them
and the street erects its shadows.
I orbit the flat, itinerant as light.

The Shining Fleet
for Philip Hodgins and Peter Porter

Like your shining fleet those remnants shone,
angles on goldlessness anvilled in agony.
Pyramidic to some, historic banks to others,
they loom like vanished communities,
empires of detritus sprouting pepper-tree
and finite gum. What's left of tested gold
is arid carpentry and cyanide,
a broken rib-cage rusting in the sun.
Piranesi's arch lingers on this nullity:
putative snakes, a Clydesdale cantering away.
Now the only visitants prospect on Sunday,
fossickers with alien tools, forlorn,
dogless even, waiting for rain to gouge
a golden path—easy money, resurrection.
Some triumphs take a tenderer turn,
past the creek beautifully reeded,
mounting mullock heaps mercurially,
scratching and clambering into glory,
a kind of glory random in the sun,
as our host, moving ahead, negotiates
a dirt gully, sliding as we stumble,
riding on the known like a bony surf,
lucid and weightless in the ashen air.

Homonym

No one answered the telephone like that:
a brief pause, the infectious lilt,
giving gossip a good name.
When I write to your widow,
groping for a phrase,
it is your name I scratch on the envelope.
At the wake everyone calls each other Philip,
the ABC interviewer mistakes me for you,
keeps doing it, has to stop.
The silence is more plausible than my halting eulogy,
the vigil of the sheep at the Timor cemetery
more eloquent than this.
Your *LRB*s are mounting on the fridge.
What will I do with them?

Hitler Weather

Strangely it shines on
those paladins and travesties,
the pantomime snaking
through swastikaed streets,
dignitaries eyeing each other
in a stand, anxious to see
what so-and-so is wearing,
whose ear Hess cultivates.
Oddly persistent like a BBC summer,
sunlight intensifies its backdrop,
the same plausible Munich,
caught beautifully in 1938,
the same respectable débutantes,
now cardiganed and matronly,
skin taut or curiously wrung—
hilarious, full of mockery.
What *does* she look like in that dress,
and what extraordinary weather
he brought them, seemed to bless.
They are laughing in the stalls;
the horror hasn't happened and when
it does they will sternly evanesce.
We too have our providential summers,
rows of Friday to furnace an affair.
The girls are trooping in a garden,
perfect-limbed, idly blonde,
wafts of scent for Grecian rites.
That fountain will survive any
calamity you name, sprinkling
not ideology but happiness,
while godlings in the stalls,
supremely spared, view it
as some ropy family saga,
follies of the Nibelungs:
club-foot, bull-whip, a cicatrice.

Still panting, statisticians
fade away, hide. No one
comments on an absence,
dismisses it as venial,
mere lunacies of fashion,
a hiccup in the weather.

Arguments of Rain

Slow arguments of rain.
A freshly killed possum
shivers among the woodchips.
Blossom hangs down, wet.
Going out, not sure why,
punctual joy succeeded by habit,
I pass a tenant from another flat—
the Cagney-like one who
scribbles ferocious messages,
addresses the world as 'you guys'
from beneath baseball caps.
She's standing in a courtyard,
never so rigid, so quiet.
I recognize her companion
despite the lowered head,
the rictus of sadness
that makes you look away.
Something is being imparted,
blunt as morning dialogues of rain.
My neighbour, born to the leather,
must tell the hirsute one
she is not wanted upstairs
and why she cannot be admitted.
Her tenure has expired,
the drizzle seems to say.
It is a banal message, never
well expressed, but often told.
Then grace notes of disbelief,
something terrible welling up,
some primal doubt or fear,
and the outcast is pulling her hair,
sick of it, impatient.
We have all heard the wailing
that will surely follow.
We have all been woken at night

and listened, complicit.
Returning with my newspaper,
forced to pass them again
and the witnessing possum, knowing
precisely which text they're using,
which lesson they're up to,
I scuttle past, climb the stairs
two, three at a time.
My high window overlooks
the horrible comedy. From above
it's like a slaughterhouse,
the possum saturated,
the rain settling in for Sunday,
the two of them hopeless, dejected.
How long before my neighbour,
remotely bored, calls a halt,
says she must go now?
Upstairs, aggressively naked,
we listen in silent sympathy
befitting our first night, first morning,
lips moving only in a kiss,
resisting slow arguments of rain.

Aubade

And I felt something of that old breeze
sloping through aquatints of morning,
wielding comb-like implements of dawn.
Or was it some specious talk of angels,
fulminations of cynics, sages,
that ministered to this historic, far-off music,
raising me a faithful of morning,
its burdens, its shadowy insight,
if only sunlight catching the lower rungs
of a ladder leaning without intent
as in a Hopper evocation
of something comparably past—
or the meditative movements of a house painter
loping through silken depths of morning,
aware of part of himself, choric and unattainable,
veering out in a retinue of cypress?

Roman Blinds

It's as if we waited all morning
for this yelp of the notorious,
fissures of day with its
expensive, arcane instructions.
But was it worth it in the first place?
It's just another aleatory Saturday,
catchy, fervid, pompously lit,
everyone drifting off in summer poses,
wondering when to winch up the slack,
the blinds, the superannuation.
Traumas of traffic sustain
through gulpings of morning.
After the several cups of coffee,
the wiggings, the pastry moments,
let's curl up in a world
sane and commodious
as thinking film criticism.

Self-portrait in Non Sequiturs
for Brian Henry

Whose damn birthday are we celebrating anyway?

That's one way to make a pass without being suggestive.

Those daguerreotypes can't help us now.

Do you want it in Italian?

Joseph has so far to go, they shake their heads in Marketing.

She places it beautifully, don't you think?

I'll be in the library if you need me.

Such a docile expression I had never seen.

Must we have the whole orchestra in black?

Weekends, the entire house was decked in flowers,
    even rooms where no one goes.

So much for silent numbers.

The hands of a saint, if you know what I mean.

I can get it for you wholesale.

You'll hurt yourself doing it that way.

Too many quotes, too many footnotes altogether.

My last glimpse of him was in a mirror. Imagine.

Leaving Prague

That beautiful instant when the sun,
renowned behind suggestive snow,
rocking like a rhythmic train
aptly named the Carl Maria von Weber,
emerges in a luminous silence
like something amplified and *faux*—
while he, sitting opposite,
the Czech boy with his dozy text,
distended legs, wakens from furrowed sleep
(the exam he is condemned to sit,
town or romance hurriedly left),
opens those grey explicit eyes
as if transformed by morning
thinly rising over revenant Dresden,
smuggled into a blue future,
handsome, lightful, without a past.

The Hotel Misericordia

Unable without emotion
to so much as glance at
a particular street number,
compute so many thousand lira,
I skirt the Anno Domini
like tourists bound for catastrophe,
crimson harvests specious as cloud,
quaint villages strewn in a quake.
Old sequences,
old talismans prevail—
the year two people parted,
abject, with a handshake.

Where are you?
Where are you now?
I am there already,
ten years hence,
that place we swore
we would never visit,
stasis, responsibility,
dystopia's present tense.

Serendipitous are faded rooms,
Rome's anodyne remonstrance,
antiquity's revenge.
The same room,
the same bed even.
The light has barely shifted
on the floor. A chair
is where you left it,
to insult or be struck.
No one flounders at a secretaire.
Dust falls with domestic economy,
sacred songs of doubtful piety.
Then the bed on which we drowsed

late into the morning,
legs inter-choreographed.
Drowsed and dreamed
cisalpine schemes—
A woman bringing coffee
in broad white cups
lacked features
and a scruple.

Unable without emotion to glance
at a particular street number.

If lovers break down in a farther room
it is not us they bury,
nor us they choose to mourn.
And there is no solace
in a logic of remembrance.

Magnolia

Boy, with your huge brown Velázquez eyes,
your consummate way of dipping them
like the expensive brushes you try to sell me
though not really trying; with your
Marine haircut and Adamic complexion
on which the coastal blush fades,
ashamed to mar such Latin perfection;
with your ledge-like shoulders and
mail-order forearms, your staunch way
of standing with certain masculine customers:
I memorize you as you memorize my order,
lazily, fitfully, like an Italian waiter
looking up to verify a seventh time,
spurting pastels in a litre can of
domestic white; memorize each muscle
in your back and in your thigh
as you autograph then hammer on the lid,
activate the Tudor contraption
like a slapstick cocktail;
follow the adventures of your placid pulse
as you cavort with the shop's Alsatian,
taut manhood briefly fond, forgetting itself;
know you as you calculate the sum
with an ironic and flickering tongue.
Exchanging one last encyclopedic look,
I accept your receipt, accept also
the casual invitation proffered
like a bonus, like an afterthought.
Back home, admiring your stylish 'Magnolia'
slashed on the lid, I try to remember
Genet's theory of curveless calligraphy
espoused years ago in Rome by a forerunner.

Shuttle

The light plane switches off like a wasp,
an abrupt piece of farm equipment.
It is all over in a few seconds,
surprising peace after turbulence.
The casualties are luggage
spilt on the tarmac like opalescence.
The steward stops barking at us
and the windows fill with purposing.
The capital is frigid,
the concourse an apathy of suits.
And you're not there.

Indian Giver

A smudgy plinth
bowered in roses.
How they tangle,
even as they moralize.

Your breath on my shoulder,
avid for narrative.

The cord you fixed once,
rolling a sleeve.

A volume of death-masks.

That night you went into the attic—
I forget why,
who forgets nothing.

A window-box
installed one summer—
barren now
except for relics of rosemary.

One object you took back
to give to another,
ever practical.

There are moons
wherever you look,
not all perfect,
and men at darkened windows
in their shirt-sleeves.

Sitting Ducks

How delicate, the translator.
Can you think for him? she cranes,
sensibly clothed against memory,
springtime knottings and burrs.
Can you feel for him?—
statistics in a light plane
casting a dubious shadow.
Glamorously the sun disappears,
though we expect more, always,
and copious moons to filigree doubt,
doubt that haunts like a mohair self.
Beauty has so far to go,
so much to tell us.
Now it leads us round the lake,
who are deaf sometimes, and fractious,
as any body of water is
shored with a variety of injuries,
complicit, fond of self-pity.
Happily, these bundles of birds
replicate the longest necked,
dipping when they do,
bobbing through history.
Like sequent poplars they blacken.
Pines too take their time,
alternating in sighs.
Pastels by the water deepen
into significance, a new ennui—
those tenuous, eventual conditions:
progenity, or any twilight.

Amphitheatre

No one has performed in this space
until now. No one has needed to.
Day's commerce frantic and done,
midnight observes its own latitude,
acoustics like a memoried bliss.
Ours is the first performance.
We have created these roles
in the towers of memory.
Promptless and unlit we dawdle,
the audience alien and otherwhere.
Concentrated in you, I am
your raptus, your ovation. Silent,
I lay down my glasses, my score,
mark you in the whirling darkness.

Quartet

All day, I don't know why,
I long for cigarette as a canny novelist
craves dirty sex to swell a scene,
the hero rifling through laundry.
It's in the contract,
panaceas claused in tar.
We signed, we have our witness,
the eventual moon contradicting
a child's impossible shadow,
idlings on a loveless platform
etched on the century.
Rhetoric of destiny fails to dissuade,
nor the livelong anecdote
you will us to sustain
like some long-breathed melody.
The grass is snaked and poemed by turns,
the crossing fitly perilous.
Afternoon briefs us with four dead lambs,
teasings of slaughterdom,
one for each of us, airless mascots
taken in different ways—
tenderly, with indifference,
more contentious work, then the gore.

Mitternacht

Bred myths insinuate strung night,

the way it unfolds a palpitating heart,
goads and excites,
leaves it panting on a stair,

the only song an alto prayer
heard through a wall,
sorrowing Gustav.

Soon midnight closes its novella,
the remembered, reread novella,
a pencilled aperçu absurdly dated.

Always the same lesson,
always the same sentimentally dated lesson,
memorized in the cool of the morning,
the deep Adriatic cool of the morning,

to your right,
aching in the sea,
unscalable Albania,
shoreless as mania,
turning a subtler blue.

Always the same lesson
departing from Corfu.

Now the furniture of my imagination
deranges itself, rearranges itself.

Bored by empty cycles of night and day
chronology, like a misfit,
a dope addict,

forfeits its Grecian profile
for a Socratic snub.

Nothing happens in an upstairs room,
nothing is meant to,
nothing allowed.

Dreamt roses are the more perfect,
the more inflamed.

Last night I wandered in these rooms,
found two vases of gorgeous blooms,

weighting the console where you left them,
leafing the strangeness where you set them,
you whom I never believed,
bearer of camphor and lilac,
metamorphosed as feather, eggshell.

Should your Tristan or Isolde
wake you with collect calls
from Singapore or Malaga

night will stir you with its importuning,
night will lead you out into the cool air,
fragrant with unbelonging,

how nothing is shapely or recognizable,
nothing ever the same:

neither surreal Bacchants in the lithograph,
masturbating each other
for a dilettante's dollar,
nor the stately bric-à-brac
shone for a more decorous plan.

Briefly, richly, I understand,
how the world resists a frantic hand,
buries it like contraband.

If you were to die tomorrow;
I am already gone.

Then blossom, like silver, nightfall,
graffiti on a tatty wall—
Property is bereft.

In Your Story

after Edward Albee

This obliquity is almost shining,
those eyes of a different colour.
In your story we are all triptychs,
dynasties of pearly selves,
needing so many acts to intermit
a flawed heart, the loping silence.
Cloudage, suspended or real,
ushers rancour, vindication.
Across orchestras, promenades,
immortals step onto a terrace,
admire the infinite, humanized greenery.
What curious lives they must lead
in their tumid, adulterous valleys.
Spontaneity the gods, endamaged, lack.
New perspectives, severely raked,
take our lines away, dispossessed.
In a park, day perpetrates its farce,
merchants, selling palmery,
glide backwards in their noble tans.
The children are gathering autumn.
They do not understand yet—
the falconer ignores their plight.
Your character would identify
with this sorrow, this realized joy.
The soliloquy at the end baffles
old perplexities; we ease them
with our random gait. Like Spartans
of some consummate struggle, martyrs
brandish china and speakers, veer
northward, skyward, rearward, anyways.

George and Martha

If it's kosher to regret everything,
the mere way we have of wriggling in our skins,
colouring in like temporizing lizards,
mavericks get away with purloinings
of sophomores, anchors of the commonplace
practised like stellar sideburns,
appalled clippings for the mirror's self.
Now only the pronouns coagulate,
admitting a dimple of doubt. Twenty years on,
stung by an accidental video,
I spot your jaw in George's acne scars,
recall the same puffiness at dawn,
those eyes that refused to open
until midday's elective campari.
Silenced by courses of contrition
deemed pallid in that Roman light,
we waited for the usual dulling,
the arpeggiated coupling of cynics.
Undressing you again, memory
curiously clawed and graphic,
I trace the ridges and defiles
of your pigeon chest, always reminded
of Christian Schad's 'Agosta',
hardly less insolent than yourself,
the same pedigreed denial.
We drank as much as Albee's stoic.
There was a swing too in our nightmare,
creaking as we sprawled beneath it,
so tender we had to bludgeon something,
aiming those stones of ambivalence.
All the dawn could do was incense us,
sending us solo in a whiskied world.
Now, fast forwarding, I comprehend
your genius for derivation,
most plausible in mirrors,

ardent for a kind of blunt being.
Pouncing on some further failing,
some tepid apology of mine,
you declared, 'We regret everything',
and left the house on caustic wing.
Everything you said was a quotation,
but I am quoting you still—
in wine bars, dreams' affidavits,
my own shrill tertiary suppers.

Twenty Fingers

In the end everything is called poem.
Even the repeats are briskly observed,
gymnic memory curling in the sun
like a roll of film,
those forgotten intrigues and quotations.
Now the miracle is average, easygoing.
Entering the room
with a bottle of something
conveniently priced, you assume
that the pianist must be accompanied,
such is his resonance.
The shadows, recalling
some other carnation, slip away.
Muchness, lambent and ordinary,
is all our inheritance.

Notes

Quotidian (page 10): the Society, a defunct restaurant in Melbourne.

The Governors of the Feast (page 14): a phrase in the Gospel of St John.

The Calling of St Matthew (page 16): Caravaggio's scandalously human Mary is in the Louvre. His paintings of St Matthew, a tax collector, are in the Contarelli Chapel in Rome, near Sant' Agostino, which contains another of his paintings.

U-Bahn (page 21): Albrecht Dürer, the German painter.

Caveat (page 24): *sfumato*, in painting a softened outline.

Balnarring Beach (page 33): the 'facing island' is Phillip Island.

The Glittering Prize (page 36): Harold Cazneaux and Oliver Cotton were Australian photographers; Yoko Ono exhibited some coffins in the Art Gallery of New South Wales in 2000.

Ivan Ilyich (page 37): 'The Death of Ivan Ilyich', a story by Leo Tolstoy.

Prime Minister's Grandson (page 46): Oliver and Sikes are characters in Charles Dickens's *Oliver Twist*, and Lionel Bart's musical *Oliver*. Vyvyan Holland was Oscar Wilde's second son.

Terminus (page 51): Giacamo Puccini's eponymous heroine in his opera *Manon Lescaut* has an aria 'Sola, perduta, abbandonata' before she dies in the desert.

Memorabilia (page 52): *La Nausée*, a novel by Jean-Paul Sartre. *La Force de l'âge* (or *The Prime of Life*), the second volume of Simone de Beauvoir's four-volume autobiography.

Operamanes (page 55): Country Week is a cricket competition. Bob Rose (the poet's father) played in both the 1953 and 1955 grand finals, of which Collingwood won the former. Maria Callas was the great soprano of the postwar era. 'Casta diva' is an aria in Vincenzo Bellini's opera *Norma*, 'Ah fors'è liu' an aria in Giuseppe Verdi's *La Traviata*.

The Wall (page 56): a 'blackboy', until recently a common name for a *Xantharrhoea australias*. Émile Lambinet, a French painter, remembered by Lambert Strether in a famous chapter of Henry James's novel *The Ambassadors*.

The Classicist's Birthday Tribute (page 64): *Judas*, a painting by Albert Tucker.

Fascicles for Emily (page 65): a selection from an ongoing series of poems in the style of Emily Dickinson. Rocco is the gaoler in Beethoven's opera *Fidelio*.

The House of Vitriol (page 69): St Cecilia is the patron saint of musicians; her Feast Day is November 22. *Die Tote Stadt* (or *The Dead City*) is an opera by Erich Korngold; *Hänsel und Gretel* an opera by Engelbert Humperdinck. The Florentino is a restaurant in Melbourne. Ferencz Lehár composed many operettas.

Noritake (page 80): Op Shop, a thrift or opportunity shop. *Women's Weekly*, a popular magazine. Jean Plaidy, a British historical novelist. The editor Edward Garnett wrote a short memoir of his author D.H. Lawrence. Cyril Connolly's *The Unquiet Grave* was published under the pseudonym of Palinurus. Thomas de Quincey, critic and memoirist.

The Living Archive (page 82): Elsie Rose (the poet's mother) was a singer at Mario's, a Melbourne restaurant in the 1940s and 1950s. Antonia, the consumptive in Act Two of Jacques Offenbach's opera *Les contes d'Hoffmann*, is condemned never to sing, but her mother's memory prompts her to do so, and she expires. Robert Rose, the poet's older brother, died in 1999 and is the subject of his memoir, *Rose Boys* (2001). The Warby Ranges are near Wangaratta, where they grew up. John Donne, the English poet.

Carpenter's Cup (page 87): *The Oxford Companion to Music*, by Percy Scholes, contains a series of illustrations by 'Batt' (Oswald Barrett), one of which depicts an 'introspective' Robert Schumann whistling to himself.

Vantage (page 90): Joseph Conrad, the author of *Lord Jim* and other novels.

Compact Disc (page 92): Dulcamara is the itinerant quack in Gaetano Donizetti's comic opera *L'elisir d'amore*.

Dog Days (page 94): 'Va, pensiero', a chorus in Giuseppe Verdi's opera *Nabucco*.

A Succession of Suns (page 103): Alberto Giacometti, Swiss sculptor and painter.

Bait (page 106): 'Pent up in lath and plaster', a phrase from Herman Melville's novel *Moby-Dick*.

Wart (page 107): Gianlorenzo Bernini designed the colonnade outside St Peter's, Rome. Bernard Berenson, the art historian.

'The Catullan Rag' (page 108): a selection from a long series of poems in the style of Catullus, the Roman satirist, elegist and love poet. These are not translations, and only a few draw on specific poems by Catullus. All the figures named in these poems appear in the originals.

Donatello in Wangaratta (page 134): the poet's father coached the Wangaratta Rovers. Donatello's bronze *David*, in the Bargello, Florence.

James Merrill (page 137): the American poet, who died in 1995.

The Shining Fleet (page 138): In 1995 Peter Porter and Peter Rose visited the poet Philip Hodgins not long before his death. His house in Timor was surrounded by mullock heaps from the gold-rush era.

Hitler Weather (page 140): some Nazis believed in the phenomenon of benign 'Hitler weather'. Hitler and his régime visited Munich in 1938, amid much medieval pageantry. A recent documentary brought together some of the survivors who were in the crowd.

Aubade (page 144): Edward Hopper, the American painter.

In Your Story (page 159): 'those eyes of a different colour', a phrase from Edward Albee's play *Three Tall Women*.

George and Martha (page 160): characters in Albee's *Who's Afraid of Virginia Woolf?*

Twenty Fingers (page 162): Clara Schumann once entered a room in which Brahms was performing and was so astonished by the pianism that she felt sure two people were playing.

Index of First Lines

Index of Titles

Printed in the United Kingdom
by Lightning Source UK Ltd.
103897UKS00001B/190

9 781844 710690